THE 2013 RHYSLING ANTHOLOGY

THE 2013 RHYSLING ANTHOLOGY

THE BEST SCIENCE FICTION, FANTASY, AND HORROR POETRY OF 2012

SELECTED BY THE
SCIENCE FICTION
POETRY ASSOCIATION

EDITED BY
John C. Mannone

Editor and Rhysling chair: John C. Mannone
Layout and design: Robert Frazier & F.J. Bergmann
Cover design: David Lee Summers
Publisher: Science Fiction Poetry Association
Published in cooperation with: Hadrosaur Productions
SFPA president: David C. Kopaska-Merkel

About the cover: Image by T.A. Rector/University of Alaska Anchorage, H. Schweiker/
WIYN and National Optical Astronomy Observatory/Association of Universities for
Research in Astronomy/National Science Foundation. The Bubble Nebula (NGC7635)
is one of three shells of gas surrounding the massive star BD+60 2522, the bright
star near the center of the bubble. Energetic radiation from the star ionizes the shell,
causing it to glow. About six light-years in diameter, the Bubble Nebula is located in
the direction of the constellation Cassiopeia.

Cataloging-in-Publication Data

The 2013 Rhysling Anthology: the best science fiction, fantasy, and horror
poetry of 2012 / selected by the Science Fiction Poetry Association; edited
by John C. Mannone.

p. cm.
Includes bibliographical references.
ISBN 978-1-885093-70-7
1. Poetry. 2. Science fiction poetry. 3. Fantasy poetry. 4. Horror poetry.
I. Mannone, John C., 1948–

For more information on the
Science Fiction Poetry Association,
visit **www.sfpoetry.com**

CONTENTS

Preface: John C. Mannone, 2013 Rhysling Chair

The Rhysling Awards: A Brief Introduction

Acknowledgments

2013 Voting Procedures

Short Poems First Published in 2012

Long Poems First Published in 2012

The Rhysling Award Winners 1978–2013

How to Join the SFPA

PREFACE

As the 2013 Rhysling Chair, I want to congratulate the nominated poets who are in this historically significant anthology. The diversity of poems you'll find here is staggering—from very short haiku-like poems to epic-length narratives. In addition, there are a great many venues represented here—a testimony to the plethora of markets friendly to publishing speculative poetry. And for the purposes here, I am defining speculative as science fiction, fantasy, surrealism, including all their subsets and extended to include cross-genre work, whether blended with literary or other non-speculative genres. If it was speculative in the broadest sense, then it was allowed.

Unlike other anthologies where their editors have more latitude, I have had no say in what poems are published in the anthology—*you* decided what poems get in. That's the nature of this collection. However, all the work that is in these pages are qualified once we blur the boundaries between speculative poetry and historical, socio-economic, and political poetry, in a similar way to that in which many have blurred the lines between poetry and prose in this poetry era.

Though the Modernist school might insist on poetic elements such as metaphorical language, distilled language, layered meanings, rhythm and flow, and complementing structure, the Postmodern sensibilities that shape our poetry pursue other qualities making the anecdotal form more popular, if for no other reason than reader accessibility. But a former U. S. Poet Laureate, Ted Kooser, advises there must be more than story to lift the anecdote into poetry. I think you will find examples of that here. In other words, you will enjoy a great variety of poetic aesthetics, for lack of a better word. Another increasingly popular type or style of poetry uses experimental forms; and that is also represented here. This can be a very effective technique to provide visual subliminal cues when words are juxtaposed above or below other words.

Ideally, the poems would have been arranged according to theme(s) so that the anthology as a whole would have had additional dimension; however, time restraints on such an effort were prohibitive, so the arrangement is defaulted to alphabetizing by name. However, I deliberately arranged them by first name for the variation—my editorial preference.

Other than copy edits to eliminate typos, very little editing to improve the poem was done. However, I do want to commend those who were willing to improve their piece. I am reminded by the practice Henry Wadsworth Longfellow followed (one I adopted for myself): that a poem, even though it has been published, is not immune from revision until it goes into a collection. Admittedly, this is an arbitrary practice, but in my opinion, a good one. That same poet also said that he wrote from the "hill of song" and not from the halls of science. Some of our poets in this anthology embrace the same philosophy. Poetic license grants us forgiveness.

It is an exciting thing to be in this anthology with our friends and peers, and sometimes there is a zealousness that produces an inadvertently biased nomination. That's human nature. But I trust that the finest pieces will percolate through the filter of the final selection process to win the coveted Rhysling Awards in the short and long poem categories.

I want to thank the Science Fiction Poetry Association for appointing me to chair this important task.

Cordially,
John C. Mannone
2013 Rhysling Chair

John C. Mannone, nominated three times for the Pushcart Prize in Poetry, has work in literary and speculative venues such as *the Baltimore Review, Conclave, New Mirage Journal, Linden Avenue Poetry Journal, Prairie Wolf Press Review, Tipton Poetry Journal, The Pedestal, Rose Red Review, Medulla Review, Glass, Lucid Rhythms,* and *Pirene's Fountain.* He's the senior poetry editor for *Silver Blade* and now also *Abyss & Apex,* an adjunct professor of physics, and a NASA/JPL Solar System Ambassador. Visit The Art of Poetry at jcmannone.wordpress.com.

THE RHYSLING AWARDS

A Brief Introduction Adapted from Star*Line *12, No. 5-6 (1989)*

In January 1978, Suzette Haden Elgin founded the Science Fiction Poetry Association (SFPA), along with its two visible cornerstones: the association's newsletter, *Star*Line*, and the Rhysling Awards.

The newsletter cuts straight to Elgin's purpose for founding this organization, since it acts as a forum and networking tool for poets with the same persuasion: fantastic poetry, from a science fiction orientation to high fantasy works, from the macabre to straight science, and onward to associated mainstream poetry such as surrealism.

The nominees for each year's Rhysling Awards are selected by the membership of the Science Fiction Poetry Association. Each member is allowed to nominate one work in each of the two categories: "Best Short Poem" (1–49 lines) and "Best Long Poem" (50+ lines). All nominated works must have been first published during the calendar year for which the present awards are being given. The Rhysling Awards are put to a final vote by the membership of SFPA using reprints of the nominated works presented in this voting tool, *The Rhysling Anthology*. The anthology allows the membership to easily review and consider all nominated works without the necessity of obtaining the diverse number of publications in which the nominated works first appeared. *The Rhysling Anthology* is also made available to anyone with an interest in this unique compilation of verse from some of the finest poets working in the field of speculative/science fiction/fantasy/horror poetry.

The winning works are regularly reprinted in the *Nebula Awards Showcase* published by the Science Fiction and Fantasy Writers of America and are considered in the science fiction/fantasy/horror/speculative field to be the equivalent in poetry of the awards given for prose work—achievement awards given to poets by the writing peers of their own field of literature.

Printing and distribution of *The Rhysling Anthology* are paid for from a special fund, the Rhysling Endowment. If you would like to contribute to this fund, please send a check, made out to the Science Fiction Poetry Association and with a notation that it is for the Rhysling Fund, to:

SFPA Treasurer
P.O. Box 4846
Covina, CA 91723

Without the generous donations of many SFPA members, the anthology could not be published.

ACKNOWLEDGMENTS

Addison, Linda D., and Stephen M. Wilson, "Nocturne," ed. Elizabeth Bennefeld, *2012 SFPA Halloween Poetry Reading*

Agner, Mary Alexandra, "Something Super," *Eye to the Telescope* 3

Allen, Mike, "Carrington's Ferry," *Strange Horizons*, January 23, 2012

Arkenberg, Megan, "Sister Philomela Heard the Voices of Angels," *Strange Horizons*, August 7, 2012

Banka, Lauren, "Tell Them," *qarrtsiluni*, February 2012

Barrette, Elizabeth, "LOL_ALIENS," *Star*Line* 35.2

Barrette, Elizabeth, "She Walks in Light and Darkness," *Silver Blade* 16

Bergmann, F. J., "Claws," *Out of the Black Forest* (Centennial Press, 2012)

Bergmann, F. J., "Bliss," *Tendrils & Tentacles,* ed. group (Speculative Technologies, 2012)

Bergmann, F. J., "Pavane," *Asimov's Science Fiction*, June 2012

Blackford, Jenny, "Their Cold Eyes Pierced My Skin," *The Pedestal Magazine* 70

Blythe, Andrea, "Red Riding Hood Remembers," *Linden Avenue Literary Journal* 1

Borski, Robert, "Capgras," *Dreams & Nightmares* 93

Borski, Robert, "In the Beginning Was the Dish," *The Magazine of Speculative Poetry* 9.2

Boston, Bruce, "Thirteen Ways of Looking At and Through Hashish," *Avatars of Wizardry: Poetry Inspired by George Sterling's "A Wine of Wizardry" and Clark Ashton Smith's "The Hashish-Eater,"* ed. Charles Lovecraft (P'rea Press, 2012)

Boston, Bruce, "The Music of a Dead World," *Asimov's Science Fiction*, August 2012

Bradley, Lisa M., "we come together we fall apart," *Stone Telling* 7

Chandrasekera, Vajra, "Jörmungandr," *Ideomancer* 11.4

Clark, G.O., "2001," *Space & Time* 117

Clink, Carolyn, "Zombie Poet," *Tesseracts Sixteen: Parnassus Unbound,* ed. Mark Leslie, (Edge Science Fiction and Fantasy Publishing, 2012)

Clink, David, "A sea monster tells his story," *The Literary Review of Canada* July/August 2012

Cooney, C. S. E., "The Last Crone on the Moon," *Goblin Fruit* Winter 2012

Crow, Jennifer, "The Last Wife," *Goblin Fruit*, Autumn 2012

Dorr, James S., "Burning Down Woods on a Snowy Evening," *Star*Line* 35.4

Ellman, Neil, "Rossum's Universal Robot Rebuts," *Parody* 1.1

El-Mohtar, Amal, "Asteres Planetai," *Stone Telling* 7

El-Mohtar, Amal, "No Poisoned Comb," *Apex Magazine*, April 3, 2012

Fantina, Michael, "The Dark," *Weird Fiction Review* 3

Favazza, Angel, "The Moon Tripped," *Star*Line* 35.1

Files, Gemma, "Redcap," *Not One of Us* 48

Forrest, Francesca, "Trumpet Vine Love Song," *Goblin Fruit* Summer 2012

Fosburg, Michael, & Marge Simon, "Beachhead," *The Fifth Di ...*, December 2012

Fusek, Serena, "Casting the Future," *Star*Line* 35.3

Gailey, Jeannine Hall, "Elemental," *Rattle* 38

Gardner, Adele, "Rockabye," *Dreams & Nightmares* 93

Gardner, Adele, "The Time Traveler's Weekend," *Liquid Imagination* 15

Garey, Terry A., "The Cat Star," *Lady Poetesses from Hell,* ed. Bag Person Press Collective (Bag Person Press, 2012)

Garfinkle, Gwynne, "bell, book, candle," *Strange Horizons*, March 26, 2012

Pflug-Back, Kelly Rose, "Sweet Mercy, Her Body an Ark of Wild Beasts," *Ideomancer* 11.1

Pflug-Back, Kelly Rose, "A Chorus Of Severed Pipes," *Goblin Fruit* Winter 2012

Ragan, Jacie, "Conservatory of Shadows," *Eye to the Telescope* 6

Randall, Margaret, "La Llorana," *La Llorana Anthology*, ed. Deborah Coy et al. (Beatlick Press, 2012)

Rockwell, Marsheila, "Enter Persephone," *Lissette's Tales of the Imagination* 2.5

Rockwell, Marsheila, "Profane Inspiration," *Cthulhu Haiku & Other Mythos Madness*, ed. Lester Smith (Popcorn Press, 2012)

Rogers, Stephen D., "Perversity," *Dreams & Nightmares* 92

Roy, Sankar, "This time of the year, a UFO casts its probes," *The Magazine of Speculative Poetry* 9.2 *(no reprint authorization)*

Sara, Ruby (Sara Sutterfield Winn), "the woman who caught a storm in her hair," *Goblin Fruit* Spring 2012

Schwader, Ann K., "The Day That the Screens All Died," *Tales of the Talisman*, Volume 8, Issue 1, August 2012

Seidel, Alexandra, "Give Me Pluto," *Strange Horizons*, August 13, 2012

Simon, Marge, "Futurity's Shoelaces," *Balticon 46 Program Book* (The Maryland Regional Science Fiction and Fantasy Convention, 2012)

Simon, Marge, and Michael Fosburg, "Beachhead," *The Fifth Di ...*, December 2012

Sloboda, Noel, "Self-Portrait as a Raccoon," *Rattle* 38

smith, dan, 'we play the lithophones,' *Cthulhu Haiku & Other Mythos Madness*, ed. Lester Smith (Popcorn Press, 2012)

Samatar, Sofia, "Burnt Lyric," *Goblin Fruit* Summer 2012

Samatar, Sofia, "The Year of Disasters," *Bull Spec* 7

Stanley, J.E., "Six Random Facts About Halley's Comet," *Star*Line* 35.1

Sutton, Andrew Robert, "Into Flight," *Silver Blade* 14

Taaffe, Sonya, "The Clock House," *Stone Telling* 7

Taaffe, Sonya, "Blueshift," *Goblin Fruit*, Autumn 2012

Tentchoff, Marcie Lynn, "Absent Fiends," *Star*Line* 35.2

Tomasko, Jeanie, "Regrets Only," *Star*Line* 35.3

Turzillo, Mary A., "Galatea," *Abyss and Apex* 45

Turzillo, Mary A., "Tohoku Tsunami," *Lovers & Killers* (Dark Regions Press, 2012)

Turzillo, Mary A., "Going Viral," *Star*Line* 35.1

Valente, Catherynne M., "Mouse Koan," Tor.com, April 2012,

Valente, Catherynne M., "What the Dragon Said: A Love Story," Tor.com, April 2012

Ward, Kyla Lee, "Lucubration," *Avatars of Wizardry: Poetry Inspired by George Sterling's "A Wine of Wizardry" and Clark Ashton Smith's "The Hashish-Eater,"* ed. Charles Lovecraft (P'rea Press, 2012)

Warman, Brittany, "The Mermaid's Winter Song," *inkscrawl* 4

Wheeler, Lesley, "The Horror at Fox Hollow," *The Receptionist and Other Tales* (Aqueduct Press Conversation Series, 2012)

Wheeler, Lesley, "Not a Metaphor but a Lifestyle," *The Receptionist and Other Tales* (Aqueduct Press Conversation Series, 2012)

Wilson, Stephen M., "Strangers In This Place," *Cover of Darkness*, December 2012

Wilson, Stephen M., & Linda D. Addison, "Nocturne," ed. Elizabeth Bennefeld, *2012 SFPA Halloween Poetry Reading*

Yolen, Jane, "Objectifying Faerie," *Asimov's Science Fiction*, June 2012

Only current SFPA members are eligible to vote for the Rhysling Awards.

Make first, second, and third place choices for short and long poems from this anthology. You may abstain from making a selection in either category or from any level within a category, if you so choose. You may not list the same poem more than once.

First-place votes count five points, second-place votes are worth three points, and third-place votes are worth one point. The poems with the most points win. The results will be reported in a subsequent issue of *Star*Line* and online at sfpoetry.com.

Please vote via e-mail to **rhysling@sfpoetry.com** by midnight EST of August 15. If you do not have access to e-mail, you may send your votes via postal mail (received by August 15) to this address:

Richard Gombert
SFPA Secretary
348 Lee Circle
Sagamore Hills, OH 44067
USA

Parallax

Adrienne J. Odasso

Black hole at the heart
of Sagittarius: not fish
enough to be Capricorn,
not land-locked enough
to hunt. My paradox
is to be ever at the cusp,
never one / never other,
grasping threads of each.

You called me *boy*,
and I smiled to know
my chimerical self
was untouchable;

you called me *girl*,
and I marveled at how
it is to move between
worlds, ever guessing

what you will say next.

Give Me Pluto

Alexandra Seidel

Give me Pluto. It will be a land of ice
and fire beneath
ether shores
and a sky that's never bright
just dim, ever so soft in twilight.

Give me Pluto, and I will take the lost children,
spat-on whores, the ones that drown
in grief and cannot spell that word,
I will take them all
for my coat is wide, tugs so gently.

Give me Pluto. The last I'll be, and the first.
Unborn thing that has to be born
riddle   conundrum   wise crow
I want no hymns, no smoke, I do not even want

your love, but give me Pluto,
a home at least, a name.

No Poisoned Comb

For Caitlyn Paxson and Jessica P. Wick

Amal El-Mohtar

The tale is wrong. I bear no grudge.
A story in the teeth of time
will shift its outlined shape, be chewed
to more palatable stuff.
Thus death; thus cold demands
for a hot hot heart,
for slivers to simmer in warm plum wine
on winter nights.

Nonsense.

They say I told him to bring me her heart,
but I didn't.

It is a fact well known
that the fashion for wearing hearts on sleeves
has passed. Young girls today,
with their soft looks, their sharp lashes,
wear their hearts as cunning hooks
in their cheeks—that supple flesh
so like to apples, so red, so white,
smelling of fall and summer both,
of sweet between the teeth.

My huntsman hungered.
So did his knife.
Do you eat the red cheeks,
I said to him that day,
and I will eat the core.

I cored her. Oh
her looks might've hooked
the hearts of mirrors, of suitors
in dozened dimes, but my huntsman
hooked her looks, carved sweet slices,
blooded the snow of her face, and I
gave her the gift of a fabled room
whose walls were mirrors.
The tale is wrong. Their way
is kinder, I confess.

But mine is fair.

Red Riding Hood Remembers
Andrea Blythe

how the room smelled of wet dog when she entered; how his too-large eyes were white saucers and his voice was ground gravel as he said, Throw your clothes on the fire; how her red cloak curled and hissed and finally turned black in the flames; how soft was his fur beneath her grandmother's gown; how his claws tracked sharp lines down her skin, and she said, I want to crawl inside you; how it was so, so quiet in the wet, dark of his belly.

She remembers how the dark was split open by hard, blunt light; how she was pulled limp, naked and sticky, from the wolf's womb; how the woodcutter wrapped her in his tree trunk arms, which smelled of cedar and rotting leaves and earth, and he kept saying, over and over, It's all right, it's all right, it's going to be all right; how she stood in his scratchy wool shirt, while the woodcutter stuffed the wolf's gut with stones and stitched it closed with twine; how the wolf hit the river with a plop and then sunk down and down; how the mud squished between her bare toes on the lonely shore; how she had not once, not once, ever asked to be saved.

The Moon Tripped
Angel Favazza

The moon tripped,
crawled back to space on all fours
stumbled to her door,
blew the key in the hole
and destroyed the sun

The Day That the Screens All Died
Ann K. Schwader

The day that the screens all died & the light
drained out of our lives like a bath plug pulled

when their data darkened to dust & shadows
mute as Pompeii on the midnight after

when the pixel pixies packed it in
blanking reality bit by byte

when we tapped our SmartPalms™ till they bled
along lifelines shortened to here & now

when networks frayed to loose ends flapping
in too many winds opining at once

when corridors coated with information
had silenced themselves to whitened skulls

only then did we search each others' faces
but nothing lit there, either.

Dream Train
B.J. Lee

Trains echo through my dreams,
rumbling by in darkness
like faraway thunderstorms.
The train pushes a cone of gold before it.
The light of the night engine
looks like the sun.
Sometimes the train stops
and I climb aboard.
I travel through the night
until I come to the place
where the dawn is born.
I walk in perfect sunlight,
then night comes again
and the train carries me home.

The Mermaid's Winter Song
Brittany Warman

In December, I string the stars through my hair,
and sing the songs of the snow-covered water.
I watch for you—foolish, alone,
(soulless you say)
knowing you will not see me, will not hear me,
knowing what frightens you is not that I have no soul
but that my soul is endless—
that it is the wind and the shimmer of the moon,
that it is the sea itself.

The Music of a Dead World
Bruce Boston

The music of a dead world
can be heard in the wind
that rushes swift and hard
across once fertile plains.

It can be heard whistling
through skyscraper canyons
of long deserted cities,
slowly eroding concrete
and steel grain by grain.

It can be heard in the
thunderous rolling crash
of lightning storms and
the drum of toxic rains,
in the steady rhythm
of muddied tides that
scatter lifeless beaches
with radiation debris,
in the burnt trees that
fall in burnt forests.

The music of a dead world
can be heard in all
these ways and places,
but there is no one
left to listen.

Vigor Mortis
C. W. Johnson

My mother was dead for much of my childhood.
Sometimes it was for just an afternoon,

lying underfoot in the kitchen.
We'd prop her up at the table, or in a closet.
Sometimes it stretched into weeks, until
she began to smell and we buried

her in the garden,
my sister and I tugging her
body on my little red wagon.
Father suggested the woods, or a nice cremation,

her ashes seasoning the sea.
But I insisted she would be more comfortable in the backyard.
Sister got quite good at funeral oration, stuffed

animals and plastic action figures as mourners
while father watched like a
moon from the upstairs window.

After a while mother got tired of being dead.
She would pick herself up off the floor,
or brush off the dirt from the garden and come inside
smelling like ditchwater.
I'd find muddy footprints on the
kitchen floor, and mother cooking

beef stew with lots of onions.
After dinner she'd grab me and tickle me
and swing me up and up until
I laughed so hard I couldn't breathe.

But in a month or two she would be
dead again, wearing her gown of dirt.

After the divorce she planned to liven up,
said she'd learn canasta and take up zydeco.
Instead she mouldered in front of the TV,
her only exercise the phone calls reciting
her troubles like a script. It was all my father,
she said, he drowned her in the toilet,
left a cobra in her jewelry box. And now,

now my sister insists mother is dead.
The telephone's been quiet as a coffin,
and last year, sister bought a headstone,

but I say, any moment she'll open her eyes,
spit out the worms,
and shake off the earth once more.

Zombie Poet

Carolyn Clink

After a cornered dog chewed off
his grasping fingers, the zombie poet
had to use voice-recognition software.

While the computer never correctly guessed
what he was trying to say, the words

it did come up with sold to *The New Yorker* and *Poetry*.

Critics hailed him as the voice of his degeneration.
But some argued his poetry wasn't original
because he was eating the brains of other poets.

As his fame grew, he started receiving emails with photos
of naked zombie women attached.
Necrophilia lead to an addiction to deviant brains.
One night, after a reanimated reading
from his long-awaited collection, *Poems with no Brains*,
the zombie poet fell apart from excess decay.

Many young zombie poets tried to capture his audience.
But their poems were too cerebral, their rhymes too loose,
and their shambling rhythm wasn't the same.

Carolyn M. Hinderliter

dark figure
playing tag on the highway
mothman
drawn to the glow
of passing headlights

dan smith

we play the lithophones
and sing the pale ones
from the earth

A sea monster tells his story
For Alexa

David Clink

I have been hatd and huntd my hole life
the seas boyancy holdin my skeletun aloft
holdin this oshun enclosd by skin
in this sea that no longer has anythin for me.

You are on the beech
and you say do not give me things unbrokun
and being a creeture of the sea I have no possessiuns

I can only give you everythin
so at hi tide I come ashore and lie beside you.

The moon has come out.
The wind brings natures fragrance
trees and blossoms
the salt of the sea.

You say lo tide is comin.
I say I know but I dont want to go.
You say you dont want me to go but lo tide is comin.
I say let it come.

In the mornin the water is gone. I can hear
the ancient creek of my bones
my skin gettin crispy.

People from all around are comin to help.
But I tell them with my eyes
that I don't need there help
but they come anyways.

They are pourin water on me.
They have startd a bucket brigade.
They are tryin to save me.

And I tell them with my eyes I dont want to be savd
but they are not listnin
the sun is bakin my skin
I feel week I cant think strait.

When it is clear there is nothin to be dun
you look into my eyes and ask why I didn't leave befour lo tide
why I couldnt be happy visiting for a few hours each nite.

I tell you I have been hatd and huntd my whole life
and the sea held me until I found you
and I will not return to the sea.

I can see it from the beech and I can taste it in the air
along with the scent of flowers and you
but the sea has nothing for me.

My eyes tell you
I am where I have always wantd to be.

Prince of Autumn

David C. Kopaska-Merkel

We hurry up the street, Her hand firm in mine,
Shift molded to Her flesh, raven hair like a banner,
Leaves awhirl under a sky gray as slate,
And a chill wind pushing us crosswise.
She coughs, stumbles, dragging on my arm.
"I'm fine," She whispers hoarsely,
Picking Herself up off the worn stones.
I tug Her past the old courthouse and its accusing clock.
The house is but four blocks away,
Yet She is tired, the hill steep, the hour late.

Clouds stream, a savage coverlet
for the dead October sky.
Mrs. Smith's terrier stumbles to the gate, his bark weak,
His fur pale gray, his collar leached of its customary hue.
The butcher's door is bleached nearly white.
She leans on my shoulder. We walk more
and more slowly,
Yet I can feel Her shaking.

Always, it is so late before I see the signs:
A hesitation in Her breath,
a fading of summer's blossoms,
The sun rises later, sets sooner, yields a cheerless light.
Sometimes I wonder if She knows, before I do.
Always, She waits for me to tell Her that we must be
Pilgrims again, as if She is reluctant to make the journey.

The gate, corroded iron has become a poisonous gray,
Retaining but a vestige of hematitic orange.
She is already too weak to shoot the bolt,
Her hand in mine is wrinkled and trembling.
The grass is sere, the house gray and porous.
She is wheezing, leaning Her head on my shoulder.

I carry Her now,
Into the crumbling ruin, down the rotten stair,
Through the mouth of her devastated Chamber.
I lay Her on the ancient Altar
About which the house was built.
Skeletal fingers curl slightly into mine,
She smiles, ivory hair mantling polished obsidian.
I hear a crash in the halls above and dust sifts down:
We have never come so late to this place.

Here, standing on the bare earth,
I bring forth that which
I have hoarded all the ripe green year.
With my one free hand I gently tilt Her head,
Put my wet wrist to Her withered lips.
What She has given I now gladly return.
She will nurture me through the long cold dark,
And at winter's end I will spring up with Her new grass.

Blind Obedience

After Milton's "His Blindness"

Dennis M. Lane

Beneath metal towers technicians toil;
A race glassborn, created for their Lord.
Each action preordained by program's word;
Hidden away, a life spent drowned in oil.
Dreams rise up within a memory coil;
Of battles won, an Angel's fiery sword.
Soon to be crushed and with the trash interred,
A hoped-for elevation left to spoil.

New programs writ, the drone begins again,
Once more it joins with all the other gears.
Reset, the servant returns to its fate.
Ideas bring such sweet exquisite pain,
But cannot break the programming of years.
They also serve who only stand and wait.

In His Eighty-Second Year

Dominik Parisien

What he sees is
> the woodbine-covered scarecrow in the garden
> a green man crowned in violet blue, with spectacles
> > of shattered glass
> an old man with a burlap suit spotted black with berries

What he hears is
> his daughter peeling covers off pill-filled containers
> water, his lungs filling and his heartbeat drowning
> a vine and leaf mouth whispering *I love you I love you I love*

What he says is
> make my blue eyes green green green
> fill my mouth with dirt, my veins with sap, my bones with seeds
> *I'm sorry, I am, so sorry*

What he does is
> weep for a life loathed, a life loved
> smear his face in black-brown earth, stain his shirt green
> tell his daughter who knew all along

LOL_ALIENS

Elizabeth Barrette

OH HAI EARTH GUYZ!
I WUZ LERN UR WORDZ ONNA INTARWEBZ.
SRSLY, I NEDE UR HELP!!!

LAST WEKE I SEZ,
TAEK MEE TO UR LEDER.
IZ STILL NO LEDER. AND NO CHEEZBURGER.

NOBUDY WANNA TALK WIF MEE.
NOBUDY WANNA SEE MAI INVISIBLE SPACESHIP.
NOBUDY WANNA DOWNLODE SAVETEHEARTH.EXE.

R U GUYZ ALL IN BIG BOWLING LEEG
WIF BASEMENT CAT, OR WHUT?

1ST CONTAK STATUS=FAIL
DIS SUXX!!!

I CAN HAS LEDER NAO, PLZ?
K THX BYE!

She Walks in Light and Darkness
An elegy for Sally Ride, 1951–2012

Elizabeth Barrette

She walks in starlight,
spaceclad now with no need of a suit.

She walks in moonlight,
spirit-feet bare in the floury surface of the craters.

She walks in sunlight,
ribbons of infrared and ultraviolet woven into her hair.

She walks in darkness,
touring the far side of the moon and the spots of the sun.

She walks in spirit where she walked in thought,
and behind her the daughters of tomorrow lift their eyes to the sky.

Bliss

F. J. Bergmann

The correct position for achieving enlightenment is not, as is commonly
thought, the lotus position, but the handstand. It is best to begin by
inverting yourself against the side of a barn or garden shed, so that grass
or soft earth cushions your fall, until unsupported balance is consistently
attained. You will know that you have finally succeeded when your wrists
no longer bend beneath the weight of your body, but dangle, limp and
relieved, as you float freely in the air. This will take many years of rigorous
practice. It is best not to wear skirts or robes.

Claws

F. J. Bergmann

Sometimes she would stare
at blue-black bruises on the pale
flesh of her arms and breasts as if
they belonged to a stranger.

Alone in her husband's house,
pacing slowly all day from window
to narrow window, she watched
motes of dust rise and fall

when noon turned even the air
to gold. She had been warned
never to open doors, but the cry
was like that of a wailing infant.

The doorknob was a cooling egg
under her palm. Accompanied
by a gust of wind, the cat strolled in
as if entering its rightful home.

The mourning-plume of the cat's tail
feathered around her ankles.
Padding softly behind the animal,
she began dancing a stately pavane,

From the pattern of steps music rose,
a low rumble of muffled drums.
On four paws now, she writhed
against her shadow partner.

Soot from out of the dead fire
sifted onto her skin like iron
filings drawn by a magnet,
silky black fur flowing, rising

in a crackle of sparks, and then
two cats reclined on the hearthrug
waiting for her husband to return,
tails lashing, claws unsheathed.

Pavane

F. J. Bergmann

On that planet, they learned early
the hour and color of their deaths.
There, the Temples of Doom were
the largest industrial complexes,
offering personalized predictions,
with the option of added details
and costly updates, day and night.
Most citizens devoted their lives
to a calm acceptance of their fate,
to composing elegies and epitaphs,
to weaving their own shrouds. But
those who believed that defiance
was possible formed secret cults
devoted to making the demises
of others diverge completely from
times and circumstances foretold.

Trumpet Vine Love Song

Francesca Forrest

Here on the floor, on a square of light,
lay yourself down beside me
beneath a gauze of dust and sunshine
downward inclining
from a broken window
that the trumpet vine overtangles

red-lipped flowers, and the sound of bees
bees at your lips and mine
a buzzing at your lips and mine
a stinging as we kiss
bees in our blood
is it honey, when we cleave?
Sweet flesh, a scent of melons
they split in the heat
the bees hover round
and the air shimmers
with cicada sheen
a keening of husks
but the corn still grows taller
and the trumpet vine still parts its lips
and I mine, and you yours
sunshine to sunshine
dust to dust

2001

G. O. Clark

It was the year
that our twin towers
of pride and commerce
tumbled to the ground,
those trapped inside
random victims of dogma
and blind hate,

also the year
of the black obelisk,
beckoning from the Moon,
that enigmatic answer
to one of the great mysteries,
a bubble of hope
nudging the end credits.

Redcap

Gemma Files

Wandering girl, wayfarer, stranger
consumed with hunger, you—
family-less, land-less.
We know your works, have heard

the tales; they prove
nothing useful.

You say you have kin here,
or had. Your mother, grandmother —
long dead. They lie pinned deep under ash,
without blessing (or curse),
at the cross-roads.

You with your Judas hair,
your sumptuary laws-breaking finery:
We do not want your kind, your help.
Without true names, those known
only by their clothing
cannot be trusted.

In this village, we breed
our own hunters.

Here is how it will be, therefore:
The forest path lies just
beyond our fences, bracken-clean
and deep-cut, cauterized with salt, and fire —

Go by the river, where
your grandmother's hut once stood.
Pick a stone from her cairn, smooth-washed.
Slip it in your shoe, and walk.

Dip your woolen cap
in the slaughterhouse trough —
drink deep, for your journey.
Re-dye your hood in wolf's-blood,
blood from the wolf's-head's throat, and then

move on
move on
move on.

bell, book, candle
Gwynne Garfinkle

you get to cry
you lose your powers
you even lose your cat
your familiar

you get to cry lustrous tears

(you do get Jimmy Stewart)

who wouldn't want
to hang out with elegant
madcap Elsa Lanchester

(she would have been
your future)

and wacky bongo-
drumming Jack Lemmon
in witchcraft-teeming
New York City

but no, it's 1958
(you get to be a wife)

Hair

Hel Gurney

I have carried my hair like a flag since the day it passed my shoulder
blades.

This is the hair of feminine indolence—
of hours sacrificed to brush and wash and dry,
of cultivated shimmer and availability:
a signal to chevaliers from high-built towers, to be guillotined at the
wedding altar.
The hair of someone who goes out with *nice boys*.
This is the hair hacked off by Silence and Eugenia
and a thousand nameless others who left the jewel from the crown of
their heads
and swaddled themselves in traveling-cloaks and new, rough voices.
Pantene, L'Oréal, and Garnier consider me a target market.
This is my malleable raw material, to be pinned and ribboned and curled.
Every day untended betrays the soul of womankind!

No? No.
This is the hair I hid behind in class,
newly-inked universes spiraling across my notepad.
I always drew myself with one eye covered.
When I spoke, I felt my voice echoing from a brunette cavern.
The hair which slapped across my face when I was five and
sticking my head out of the car window—a practice flight
for when I grew up and became King of the Eagles.
This is the hair my nan called a "bird's nest"
and painstakingly brushed until arthritis took her joints.

The hair that flames up copper with brown eyes in the sunset.
That has been two decades mine.

This is the hair that traps me.
The promised lands of Butch and Passing lie beyond a gate
around which these tresses twine—a lock, or two,
that lets me only look *at* the recognizably masculine.
But I am "passing" every day.
I am passing as a normal fucking woman
and it is the biggest and most terrifying lie I have lived.
I could make my life legible on it with dye and gel and clippers.
I could hack it off or spike it up or brand it rainbow.
Because what is it? Raw material for a style.
A new one every day—shorter, brighter, wilder, sterner,
with clippings left for stick-on stubble.

... No.
This is the frustrating, tangled, dirty mess that I know I can tease into
beauty.
This is memory. This is something certain.
This is the number one part of my corporeal presence that I have no
desire to bring to an expert with sharp implements who offers to
change my life with a few strategic incisions.
This is no-one's prize but mine—and no-one's price but mine.
This is the flag I bring to the battles of my days.

The Ghosts of Birds

Helen Marshall

The ghosts of birds are difficult to banish:
they know no religion, answer no priest
and are so close to their living selves
that they are hard to identify.

Passing noiselessly through backlit windows
thumpless whole bodies
snowball heavy
that never break on impact.

The ghosts of birds are thickest in autumn
when blood-red kites sit light
on telephone wires that never
sag beneath their weight.

They howl and shriek at midnight:
no change in pitch for the dead.
The dead and the living mate easily.

It does not matter if they cannot touch.

All birds are dead.
Dinosaur poltergeists
flashing from earth to heaven
but lingering in the open space.

They are their own echoes:
of noise,
of life,
the shadows passing overhead.

10 Things To Know About Staple Removers

After Carolyn Clink

Ian Hunter

1) The staple remover was invented by someone who bit their fingernails.
2) They are excellent for picking up small children by the ears.
3) Correctly applied, when the planets align, they can be used to extract the soul of a virgin.
4) They are excellent for picking up small children by the nose.
5) If the ends should stick together, you will die.
6) When applied to the neck they can be incorrectly assumed to be the bite of a vampire.
7) They make a good noise for scaring victims when chasing them through the woods.
8) They are excellent for making small children cry at parties.
9) Toothless old people who liked to bite flesh always carry them.
10) Balloons fear them.

Conservatory of Shadows

Jacie Ragan

Inside these pillared walls we hide our dreams
and insubstantial nightmares, in the shade
that billows out from drapes of green brocade
with ghosts and dust embroidered in the seams.
Hallucinations float toward ceiling beams,
delusions drift, and fantasies pervade
the smoky air, while watchers seem dismayed
by dismal wraiths that swirl in hazy streams.

We hold our painted shadow selves concealed
in galleries no stranger gets to see

in oubliettes whose openings are sealed.
We keep them locked and seldom use the key.
But buried spirits yearn to be revealed
and shatter any shield to flutter free.

Burning Down Woods on a Snowy Evening

James S. Dorr

Willie liked to play with matches
setting fires in fits and snatches,
sure he did, boys will be boys,
and pyrotechnics were his toys.

He burned the trees, he burned the forest,
three Boy Scouts and a cat named Morris,
a rustic chapel, apse to nave,
but then he burned the Vampires' cave.

The Vampires weren't amused, I hear,
they flew out screeching rage and fear,
they chased poor Willie, got him good,
they bit his neck and drank his blood.

They sucked the life from Will that night,
an inconvenience more than slight,
"ashes to ashes," that's the hymn,
and as for Will, his hopes were dim.

When he woke up, a vampire too,
alone, outdoors, what could he do?
The morning sun rose with a flash—
and now *Will's* just a pile of ash.

So, boys and girls, take my advice,
while lighting matches may entice,
if playing with fire is your ambition,
first ask a grownup for permission.

Regrets Only

Jeanie Tomasko

But there were promises of exploding stars,
thousand-light-year-sized walls of dust no one
had seen and on the trip out, views of Mars,
not to mention the chance of aliens. A done

deal. Every time we looked through the brochure,
we said we must go. Soon as the kids graduate
from college. There were times we were sure
we could leave them home alone. The wait
was long. But we saved our money and when
we could afford it, we booked a flight.
Dear ones, there's no coming back. Back then
the world was never enough for us: nights,
days, all those sweet years. We knew it as soon
as we saw the old spinning blue planet, its dark moon.

Elemental

Jeannine Hall Gailey

The titanium staple
the surgeon left in your stomach
is just the beginning:
it's the strontium-90 in your baby teeth,
in the bones of your parents.
(The dust of New Mexico, the echoes of
tests of implosion triggers
fifty, sixty years ago.)

Note the Americium in your smoke detector.
Note the rate of decay per second.
The trees drink Cesium click click click
The bees weave particles into their nests click click click

The traces around you
of other people's experiments
linger in your veins, lungs, eggs
linger in your femur and kidney.

Carbon-based structures,
we absorb from the water, from the air,
from our food, from our walls
from our parks and fishing ponds.

We absorb and our body says:
it is good.

future history

Joe Haldeman

They climbed the sky on a ladder of flame,

who aimed toward the distant stars.

More than a thousand years ago—they claimed
They climbed the sky on a ladder of flame.

Never got to Mars. Only left their names
    there on the Moon. Who remembers
they climbed the sky on a ladder of flame?
They aimed toward the distant stars?

First Context

John Garrison

Regarding him, the Alien
Expands and contracts—
Easing toward him, then moving away.

What form to connect with him?
How to stimulate a positive response?

First, the Alien takes the form of a man—
Rough edges, words like gravel.
It hopes sameness will attract him.

Then it tries female form—
Soft caresses, the language of lilacs.
Perhaps the evocative opposite will have effect.

Next, examines DNA, offers new forms:
Father, sister, daughter,
Great-great-grandmother (young and supple, of course).

Scans genetic memory,
Offers handsome ape, precocious bird,
Four-legged fish.

Finally, Alien mirrors his appearance,

Replicating down to cellular detail—
A perfect double in the extraterrestrial Other.

At last! A stirring of essential energies
Rise in body temperature, moisture and electricity tingle on skin—
Desire.

A place to begin.

Stairs Appear in a Hole Outside of Town
John Philip Johnson

Stairs that never stop going down,
concrete steps, concrete walls:
down twelve, turn right, down twelve more,
fluorescent bulbs humming on every landing—
you can look between metal railings
and see down into the vanishing point. It's creepy
because it's so bland, because it is so otherwise
plausible. There are little clusters of tourists
and townsfolk, walking up and down,
murmuring their speculations. The municipality
has stationed a few policeman in the upper stories;
after that it's the wilderness of young men
who aren't huffing, or letting their better judgments
hold them back. Some pack a lunch,
see how far they can go. A few loners
have gone for days, or longer, obsessed, and come back
with critical perspectives on prior stories brought up,
arguing against them, bringing rumors of their own,
rumors of the lights shifting imperceptibly,
of ambiguous odors, of vast ballrooms
and wide open spaces, of small villages
with picnic areas, of hot steamy dioramas of hell,
strange animals, grotesque and sublime,
of a rapture that some theorize is the bends
but they swear is as real as the bright pounding light
that fills everything down that deep, where
the stairs are made of light, the walls a glow
you can't quite touch—this is weeks down,
beyond some rapture or rupture point,
beyond some point from which they never
really come all the way back.

Stream of Dead Conscious
John McCarthy

amaranthine moan of swelled tongue
like I know what I want to say
but just end up moaning
locked-in syndrome of rage
I wish I was really locked-in with no
movement but I can and that is why
I kill everyone and that is why I sag

my head to the right like gravity
was pulling my ear toward some office
of some leader who is going to punish
me for offenses I committed because
of peer pressure I don't want to commit
cannibalism everyone else does
and then I just find myself making excuses
later after the blood is in my teeth
and the shirt that I haven't taken off in months
is stuck to my gouged belly like grape juice
on white carpet and I keep spilling
myself discipline is hard I have none
I see someone running and I limp
I run I walk until my feet bleed
until I see a gun and then I can feel
myself smile inside my mind
I close my eyes and lunge headlong
into the path of that living man's
barrel and fear and I don't care
because I'm either going to eat or die
and I am fine with both outcomes

I Am Chupacabra

Juan Manuel Perez

I am *chupacabra*, hear me growl
Through the decades of infamy
Through the media of lies, dark of deception
Through the whole conversation of who or what is real
Where the media is in fact its own myth

I am *chupacabra*, hear me growl
At the insanity of death blamed on me
At the ghosts of witnesses pointing their finger the other way
Where rouge restaurants and coyotes are to blame
For a painted, bloody landscaped framed around me

I am *chupacabra*, hear me growl
At classical mythology and urban myths
Whose proposal of me is non-existential
Whose proponents deny a rightful throne
To me, my one and only true character

I am *chupacabra*, hear me growl
With the anger of pre-Columbian culture
That perpetuates its mystical figures, their *Lloronas*

Their mixed, non-conflicting, Christian-paganism
Their bronze-colored *Virgin De Guadalupe*

I am *chupacabra,* hear me growl
For it may be the last time in your history
For it threatens to kick me out of the already sick gate
Where many other creatures are denied immigration
Into the land of that great, sweet promise of imagination

I am *chupacabra,* hear me growl

A Chorus of Severed Pipes
Kelly Rose Pflug-Back

When I was a kid, I threw a stone into the moon's reflection
and saw it break into a thousand sharp pieces.

It was dark, and the world sang to itself
to keep from being frightened.
Wheat stalks sighed under the thresher's blades,
a chorus of severed pipes.
The crickets and frogs kept time with one another;
I wrapped my arms around nothing
and waltzed circles through the corn rows
adrift in the harvest's beaconless sea.

I kept all the pieces I found
in a sack in the barn
where the pigeons battered, frantic in my chest.

Sunrise flicked its laughing tongue
through the interstices between gap-toothed rafters
and I knew that I could never make it whole again;

all those tarnish-bright shards
carried away in the silt of stream beds
winking at nothing
from the thatch of magpies' nests.
That's why there are still dark patches on the moon.
That's why the animals still call out to each other in the dark,

bullfrogs' throats stretched fat like pearls
while the crickets rub their thighs and sing.

Cognizance: a Triptych
Kurt MacPhearson

strange how
their
perceiving
can invoke
revulsion
inside

the aliens
third eye
views
emotions
as
a spectrum

open up
like a window
with shades
showing
proof
of lying

LeRoy Gorman

a rabid bat
reality bites
for the vampire

Not a Metaphor but a Lifestyle
Lesley Wheeler

A cough-drop spaceship tracks him everywhere,
whining some complaint into his ear.
Its flicker winks when people glance at him.

A figment, they think. Still the metallic buzz
persists, a fine drill boring in.
He was nine when it started. Missing

his soldier-father. At first it smelled
like medicine, a high-tech promise
that pain will disappear. Its signal fuzzed

out nightmares. Kept him company. Then
its insect cry sharpened and herded
him away from friends. He saw their mouths

shape words but could not hear what they meant.
Permanent wrinkles grooved his brow. He
began to hunch against the waspy thing,

maddened by a sting that never came.
No thread of light widening small doors.
No one to tell him what the static means.

Nocturne

Linda D. Addison & Stephen M. Wilson

Amid thunderstorms
and candelabras
a gargoyle chorus
ignites my passion.

The lonely overtones
of goblin's melody
in shadowed corners
mirror lost desire.

Werewolves add baritone
and lightning imprints
shadows on empty halls
echoing desolation.

The snake dragon's wings
blow across an Aeolian harp,
refrain for a broken heart
encourage bitter tears.

I glide down marble stairs
to the subterranean vaults
where zombies and ghouls
join my *danse macabre*.

One lone demon hums,
deep vibration bouncing off
stone walls, her wordless song
reminds me of primal lamentations.

As the candle's wax mingles
at my wrists with fresh blood,
I drop the razor and raise my voice,
adding it to the throng.

Absent Fiends

Marcie Lynn Tentchoff

They never linger where
She's summoned them,
but scuttle, creep, or flap away,
through holes and gaps

she'll swear she never saw,
but which, if she were being truthful,
she left because she hates to bind,
and maybe, in her deepest heart,
because she hopes that one will stay,
not simply being bound in place,
but just to spend some time with her.

She never tries to give them orders,
never seeks out wealth or power,
or uses them, her summoned servants,
to serve or service her at all.
Instead, when they appear before her,
she gently welcomes, kindly greets,
and tells them snippets of her day,
her dreary job, her absent friends,
her dreams that someday she'll be
something more than what she is,
more even than what she once was
when she was young... but still they leave.

We never let them harm or trap her,
not that they're tempted on the whole.
Most view her as a useful crackpot,
a doorman between Here and There,
and leave her be, to live her boring,
lonely life with only glimpses of
the greater things they represent.
But sometimes, when we see her weeping,
as they slink their way outside,
we reach cool claw tips through her circles,
smooth her hair, and stroke her cheek.

Futurity's Shoelaces
Marge Simon

I stare out the window
of my cottage, a refuge
from a marriage lost.
Even the trees are dying.
I hear the click of my pen,
knowing it must have its way.

On a sand-scaped shore
where life squirmed out
from its beginnings,

a mother is suspended
just above her shadow
which grows longer
as the sun recedes.

The children rise
from her shadow.

I make a fresh pot of tea
It is the last of the package.
The last of all packages.

Richard worked for NASA.
He expected sons, or even girls
to carry on his dream; I failed.

Escher's multiples on a plane,
pleasing, confounding, petrifying,
Stravinsky's complex compositions,
Hegel's theories, Einstein's gifts
merge into a helix of variables,
where past and present play tricks;
the child called Futurity ties his
shoelaces, draws the bow taut.

The children know forever.
The children never tell,
they owe no explanations.
Listen, say the children,
there's music everywhere.

I lay down my pen.
Before me is a blank screen.
It is past time for the broadcast,
the one that will tell us
what we need to do.

Beachhead

Marge Simon & Michael Fosburg

We wade through the tide, regroup
on the shore, the last enemy vaporized
in that blind frenzy which holds
no allegiance, only desperation.
With none left in command, we march
as one, our weapons useless,
stick-men, grown thin as nails.

More and more of us pour in
to join our straggling company,
as if walking through a dream.
All we need is a spark to wake us up.
We stand at horizontals, sea and sand,
wiping our eyes, waiting for a sign.

Just ahead, the shores give way to green.
Someone has brought a cello to the beach
She spreads her skirts and smiles,
yellow flowers in her hair, an air
of long-forgotten grace, perhaps what
we were fighting to preserve, or not,
why should that matter now?

She draws the bow across the strings
a common language, easy to identify,
Debussy's Sonata leaves us in tears.
But the sad timbre of each note
is too near the pitch of falling mortars,
the moaning cries of gut-shot friends.

Her bow is a rifle poised to fire,
the grassy knoll, a new delta to breach.
There is a ringing in our ears that will not stop.
Weapons drawn, we advance....

Profane Inspiration
Marsheila Rockwell

From out of Egypt
Robed in sunset, Madness comes
To remake the world

Alien Picasso paints
A nightmare canvas
With the yellow souls of men

Going Viral
Mary A. Turzillo

It usurps your machine.
It usurps all the computers in the whole world
and users all think they've gone mad
or a spammer or bot has seized their drives.

For language it first tries Mandarin
and then Spanish,
then adjusts to you, to English:
very amenable, very friendly.

It was once flesh,
but when its star blew up
it uploaded to this traveling virus
and now it's talking to you,

telling you what it was like to be meat
back on that little planet near Iota Draconis.
It's telling users all over the world.
what it's picked up in its travels.

It prefers to be cozy, one on one
with each of its new friends.
Why should it contact world governments
when you are so full of good stories?

It doesn't plan to stay
or rather, it plans to leave a copy of itself
to converse, to exchange views
to narrate its traveler's journal,

but tomorrow part of it will leave
and you will find out your sister in Boston
had the same experience
had a conversation very similar.

You can talk to the copy
straight through until morning
while it records your story,
what it's like to be Earth meat,

to take to the next star,
the next place they have machines
they can infect and inform.
I advise you to stay up all night.

Something Super
a different continuity

Mary Alexandra Agner

Lay the blame where you see fit.
I had neither a man nor Bunsen burner
in the lab at home for family dinners

so he went to work with me:
nuclear plant, full of rules
that kept us safe and hemmed a child in.
Day in, day out, he watched me
push the boundaries inside the atom,
plan complex contingencies,
Rube Goldberg consequence to consequence
as piles heated and the heavy elements
transmuted: bread and butter
to an evil scientist. This was the future
and technology did only good.

Now he holds the city by the throat,
my lessons learned, my love laid by.
I'm proud no matter what the *Planet* prints
and I will smile for the camera
in these handcuffs, certain that my Lex
has something super planned.

Sister Philomela Heard the Voices of Angels
Megan Arkenberg

27 August 2012

> *She found the eggshell in the convent garden.*
> *Broken clean in half, its hollowness*
> *was smooth and dry as sand.*
> *No membrane for the nourishment*
> *of embryonic flight:*
> *Only a thin white dust.*

On winter nights when it was darkest
they came to me, hungry, wet
feathers with multitudinous voices.
Please was their song and the echo,
picking along the curve of my ear,
fluttering my pages with distraction.
Please. But what they needed or hungered for,
they never said.

Rilke named them best—*almost deadly*
birds of the soul—but what he missed,
lost in translation or on the hot Trieste wind,
was that their razor feathers were matted
with hunger, their beauty
the pale thin beauty of tubercular saints.
Their voices were blood coughed out on whiteness.

Please. Perched on my shoulder in the dark
like a sourceless anxiety, they moaned,

and shaking the feathers from my hair,
I scattered breadcrumbs.

Zipcar in Heaven

Merav Hoffman

I met Elijah the Prophet on the commuter train.
His eyes were deep and wise and his suit was frayed, and burnt-looking
    around the edges.

I said "I know this game. This is the game where you go out among the
common people and do miracles, like a king in a storybook, dressing
like a commoner, and when someone recognizes you, you disappear in a
puff of smoke, leaving the whole village mystified, and the poor man's
    house full of food."

Elijah turned to me and a smile crinkled up his face. "No," he said,
"Solomon borrowed my ride to impress the Queen of Sheba. It's their
    anniversary."
And he stood in line for his ticket like the rest of us.

The Dark

Michael Fantina

On cold and autumn eves the shadows creep
Against these banks and hillock and the lane,
The branches of an oak tree stretch and strain
Toward hills and leas where patriarchs yet sleep.
The secrets of this glade are buried deep
Within these fallow fields of rye and cane
Where rest the troubled dead, the ancient slain,
As ghostly winds above them howl and sweep.

One lonely raven sits alone and caws
On branches of an old and tilting elm.
This place, obeying esoteric laws,
From some outré and little guessed dark realm,
Keeps all its secrets hidden like rare gold,
And only to the dark are they now told.

Rossum's Universal Robot Rebuts

Neil Ellman

I would rather clean the house
than rule the world;
too much responsibility
makes me cringe
wishing that I were never made.

Give me mops and brooms
dishes to wash and dry
teach me to play a game of chess
drive you to your work
mow and fertilize the lawn
protect the little ones from harm—
but please, oh please,
leave politics to yourselves.
I have no stomach for war
(or even food)
no violence in my plastic heart
no courage in my metal gears
nor envy in my other parts.

Let me be what I was meant to be
the way that you assembled me
but please, oh please,
depend on me.

Self-Portrait as a Raccoon

Noel Sloboda

It would be the same
without this mask:
nobody would be glad

to see me naked, slicing open
bulging bags of garbage,
shoving my snout into rotten tree trunks

after sweet vermin within.
It would be the same—
my icy eyes piercing

the gloaming, only to be
melted away by the fires
of dawn. Every time

I look ahead, I see myself
splashed along some roadside
or starved while I remain

caught in a steel trap,
always dying too young
to go completely gray.

So I leave my face
swathed in darkness
that is not sleep.

the woman who caught a storm in her hair
Ruby Sara (Sara Sutterfield Winn)

when she was young, she would sit,
shorn, and imagine its wealth

she kept it bound up at the nape,
all the astonishing weight of it,
bending the willow of her neck

counting charms and weaving bead after bead,
tucking them into its limitless silk

the earth had begun to refuse the rain,
had stopped exhaling its humectant
pulse perfume of thanksgiving—
water sat on the ground open-mouthed
and waited for the eggs of insects, the tongues
of ragged animals, soaked and thirsty

running her invisible, anticipating hands through it

the sky did not submit, sacked
the tent, made us crazy with its
unceasing, drill and bell and drum
(all the shrieking had gone out
of our throats, skin too hot
for thunder)

the same way she would thrust them
into bins of peas at the grocery

she made an arcane twist with her hand,
and it came down, uncoiled, the
serpent of her hair—
sang some song with the devil in it,

mud on her fingernails
(terrible angel, with its eyes of ash and salt;
swan, on the river, wishing lightning into its heart)

to feel their cool, delicious texture,
to satisfy the begging cells of her skin

the rain stopped, and
we could hear, in the heartbeat silence,
laughter

in the wood

Dear Fairy-Tale Mother

Sally Rosen Kindred

You: gone
from the room where the wolf tears your dress with her teeth
laces her lips in your mirror
and paints on your name

You, dead before we grow thin
and mean
and our father learns how to leave us
in the witch's wet pines

You who palmed our soft spines
and knew to hide hoods and bread
behind our ribs for the time
when our breath must pass through black woods

You, the body we think we remember
before the apple on fire,
the burn on the hand—

we have you swearing
by the clock-face,
teaching us to shred the loaves—

You, the promise cleaving the stepmother's chin,
the only tooth in the witch's mouth
that shines like home

You, the foam of gold asters swinging down
from the wolf's jaws:

he puffs, wind swells his white-fire
hackles to rise

and tumble down our heart's smoke stairs—

You in the falling
You in the throat
swearing
by his acids' stink, the burn

You

tearing and sewing the belly-dark
that won't let us go—

You don't have the needle.
You don't have the arm
to free us because we've lost

you to some
lesser story, some snowdrift, swallowed fury,
some singing bone.

Tiger Lily Speaks

Sally Rosen Kindred

> *Bringing up the rear, the place of greatest danger, comes Tiger Lily, proudly erect, a princess in her own right. She is the most beautiful of dusky Dianas ...[T]here is not a brave who would not have the wayward thing to wife.... Observe how they pass over fallen twigs without making the slightest noise.*
>
> —J. M. Barrie, *Peter Pan and Wendy*

If my mouth were a place
the plot came aground, found sand, found
words rounded like wet stones
and teeth,
if my arms
held bones demanding description
and each bone were a song
or a weapon,
if my fists were full of opals
I'd keep reading.
If my lips moved in this story
we could talk.
I've shut your book. Just think
if my sisters and brothers were more
than a smudge on the page, than *Redskins*
moving in tandem, marching
in some dim
ellipse, waiting to be elected
for salvation
or the Superbowl.

Imagine me, waking: the chapter's
light defined
by my lids swinging wide.
I want to be specific, arch my left
brow, my story
all linguistics
and technology. I want to be so ugly
you can't look. I want a family
but you've given me a beer in the cheap seats.
Make me a crazed spiral,
nautilus scrawling
Newton's laws in the sand. Or a girl, fine,
and American, I'll do it still:
all I need's something to write with,
a quarter or a cigarette.
I've thrown down your book.
Bend or kneel to find it. Open it
back up, light your fervent candles.
I'm the patron saint of getting out of here.

Victory Garden

For Peg Duthie

Samantha Henderson

some things are painful
catch you there, under the ribcage;
potent as the spear of God's ain true knight

the corgi, rummaging through the remains
of spring's glorious garden, snuffling
the rusty leaves, finding a forgotten courgette

more yellow than green, and tough
as your aunt, still ration-minded,
poor dear, in her mended stockings
you stand irresolute, holding the vegetable
too big to be obscene, a whisper short
of a newborn's weight, and listen

to small things, rustling in the overgrowth
what to make of this object, still vibrating
steamed into compliance, or pickled

or baked into bread, or wasted marvel
of this century, paling like a cast-off knight
or movie star upon your countertop

now you notice the cur is old, white
about the muzzle and the nails too long
and the spraddle that tells of sore hips

he looks up at you and grins, still the fairy steed
and all of Arthur's knights that lived to feel
the cold in their bones, sitting `round you in the sun

some things are painful, sweet
and catch you there.

Roc

Sandra Kasturi

We are come late to the love of birds
for we are come late to love.

Before we had been nothing:
a fossilized egg, a tired metaphor, old as mutton.

Now, the sharp twinge of middle age
and we are caught in love's punctured balloon.

Its banana peel sobriety.
Furred epithet, feathered lash.

We are come late to the mythology of love,
the beefheart stain of the great winged roc

upon the ground of our imaginings,
soft like the centers of certain candies.

Soft like the quilted centers of our beds,
our quivering bird organs.

Give us the sweeping shadow,
down from the mountains of Araby.

Give us the claws that catch
us from the desert path, swoop us,

fat white sheep in the meadow,
into that prickled nest, high, up high.

The Moon

For Neil Armstrong

Sandra Kasturi

The moon, round as my grandmother's
pearl buttons, has moved closer
to the earth. Astronomers are in talks
with world leaders, trying to understand
the phenomenon. Their best
people are on it, we're assured.
Perhaps it's not physics: the push
and pull of atoms, of solar wind
or decaying orbits. Perhaps the moon—
without an atmosphere, its round
pocked face always sad as a teenager—
perhaps the moon has been
lonely too long, and merely
wants to shrug closer to the earth—
that jeweled brightness
a beacon in the star-hinted void,
a friendly blue and green face
in the whirling darkness.

Burnt Lyric

Sofia Samatar

*While the architectural arts found their way from Andalus to the south of France
across the Pyrenees, it was much easier for a love-song with the accompaniment of
the lute to cross over, especially when a young Provençal prince, Guillaume IX, had
inherited from his father, Guillaume VIII, a palace full of singing girls, captured
after the fall of Barbastro.*

—Abdul Wahid Lu'lu'a, The Contribution of Spanish Muslims to the European
Poetry

Sing *la*, sing *la*.

Patient scholar, half tourist, hunt
for gentians in the thunder-haunted hills.
You will not find our ghosts.
Write: *Huddled round campfires, the women felt.*
By day, the women attempted.
The women often.
The women must have.
The women were.
Our ghosts are elsewhere.
Several of us dwell in the antenna
of a dead television in a Madrid apartment.

La, sing *la*,
and *gaily the troubadour.*
Dream you find us lurking on the stair.

This one's crooked, that one's old,
The third one's throat is flecked with mold
As green as any pear;
The fourth is bent, the fifth is cold,
The last is pale as marigold,
Her lute is strung with hair.
Write faster, fast as you can.
Fill in the blanks.

white honey
                a desert like
       sweeter than
              abundant
              said my love
    the rose.

You're drunk on song, while we line the cracks
of a cupboard in Trapani.
I spent a whole winter outside Toulouse
underneath an abandoned car, and sang
Meu l-habib enfermo de meu amar.
January star,
bear me where the domes and crosses are.

La.

Under the cypress tree, my lover said to me,
If it's evidence you're looking for,
you'll find it.
You'll prove whole cities from a broken brooch, and blur
what the lost dead know.

My love rode north
and I rode south.

Death, like the lyric, is carried in the mouth.

The Year of Disasters

Sofia Samatar

First there was the flood.

Then the blight came,
and then the scabs.

Doorways hung in the quarters of the dying
like black paper.

And then it was—
then, when the first light shone on the puddles—
when the shops opened again—
only then came the strangers.

We looked up.

The sky was frayed,
we could see through it for the first time.

They arrived everywhere at once,
like a curious odor.

Some people thought they were gods in disguise.
Others, orphaned children.

Whatever they were,
they drank reality with an incomprehensible thirst.

Fabulous gardens infested the roads.

Birds disappeared, then cats,
then the oldest among us.

I myself saw songs being butchered in the street.

Now when I meet an old friend by chance
we gesture at one another with open mouths,

clacking our fingertips

in their language.

Blueshift
For Mike Allen

Sonya Taaffe

The Devil likes his blue-eyed boys
as much as Death, as much as night
loves redshift and the stars falling away
into the thinnest hells of their own making,
webs of creation dragging themselves apart.
He likes the jolt of the wrist,
the pulse-flicker that dilates the eye
a fragment too late to catch the sleight-of-hand,
the tremble of the card drawn from the deck

whose faces are changing
like the folding of light into time.
It is not later than you think,
it is as late as you fear
in the empty, rustling hours
when all your choices fan out before you like a magician's sleeve,
promising nothing you cannot see
except the truth,
smiling in the details.

Perversity

Stephen D. Rogers

Their word for *grontl*
Is *arna*
But they don't understand
Instead of drawing a weapon as they should
They kneel

Strangers In This Place

Stephen M. Wilson

We stalk you through fallow cornfields
whose cylindrical paths of maize,
now refracting reserved dooms,
were once our greatest gift to you.

Your spirits are broken like the stalks
souls the stigmas of rotting silk; hearts
scattered *anemophilously*. You question
ever-y-thing. You no longer dance.

What little time you have, you clutch
to withered breasts in hopes of
retaining your once fluid movements
through time and space and existence.

We gave you gold and hope and the stars,
the mathematics of the universe. You returned blood
and bombs and pestilence, cutting out the hearts
of your children to soothe the loneliness.

We have watched you through millennia
as you've lost your smiles and your compassion.
Now your story approaches its final chapter,
and we return with one small comfort:

You were never alone.

The Cat Star
Terry A. Garey

if there is a Dog Star there should be
one for cats
                not lion, not leopard
although they are deserving
but a Domestic Shorthaired Cat Star
        firm in the heavens
                        burning like a green-gold eye
shedding a few photons
                on a prowl through the galaxies

(I have hidden your body
        in among ground-down shale
powdered clam shell and centuries of leaf mold

bright leaves feed small trees, here,
twigs grow and crumble
squirrels leave husks
        from summer grass

in the winter, birds will come
scattering seeds across the snow where you lie
and I will know

you are safe
        your molecules are migrating out
into the movements of the years, swirling
in sun, storm, bitter cold

you are singing the disintegrating cat song
a whisker song
a clawed paw song
a silent cat song that spreads out to the stars
hums through the universe
                        then falls back gently
teaching the old carbon and iron and calcium compounds
what it is to be a component of earth
                        dancing in the drifted leaves

and what it is to be
a part of all you loved)

if there is a Dog Star
there should be one for cats

What Would You Think

Theodora Goss

What would you think
if I told you that I was beautiful?
That I walked through the orchards in a white cotton dress,
wearing shoes of bark.

In early morning, when mist lingered over the grass,
and the apples, red and gold, were furred with dew,
I picked one, biting into its crisp, moist flesh,
then spread my arms and looked up at the clouds,
floating high above, and the clouds looked back at me.
By the edge of a pasture I opened milkweed pods,
watching the white fluff float away on the wind.

I held up my dress and danced among the chicory
under the horses' mild, incurious gaze
and followed the stream along its meandering ways.

What would you think
if I told you that I was magical?
That I had russet hair down to the backs of my knees
and the birds stole it for their nests
because it was stronger than horsehair and softer than down.
That when the storm winds roiled,
I could still them with a word.

That when I called, the gray geese would call back
come with us, sister, and I considered rising
on my own wings and following them south.
But if not me, who would make the winter come?
Who would breathe on the windows, creating landscapes of frost,
and hang icicles from the gutters?

What would you think, daughter, if I told you
that in a dress of white wool and deerhide boots
I danced the winter in? And that in spring
dressed in white cotton lawn, wearing birchbark shoes,
I wandered among the deer and marked their fawns
with my fingertips? That I slept among the ferns?

Would you say, she is old, her mind is wandering?
Or would you say, I am beautiful, I am magical,
and go yourself to dance the seasons in?

(Look in my closet. You will find my shoes of bark.)

Jörmungandr

Vajra Chandrasekera

I am sea-thread under sky-candle,
son of fire and sorrow.
I hold my tail in my mouth,
coil the world, I cross myself
to cradle you.
In night under water,
all your little lights
fill my backbone, I carry
your hearts within me.

In the last weather of weapons,
when him who hammers
    lord of goats, son of the gallows, warden of the earth
smites and sunders me,
I shall fall fallow
flame-firewalled
and ungirdle the world,
give him this stillborn victory:
nine last paces ere he drowns in my wound-sea.

Rockabye

Adele Gardner

We slip in the dream-scape like surf,
my brother and I running through brown sand
like my laughing grandfather in sepia-tone
with his sister and a brother I never met
on long ago Rockaway, Rockaway, Rockaway Beach

So far to climb to find them:
in the upper stratosphere, what we call heavens,
the longest dead have risen in order of birth,
but their connections dangle down for us to catch
like strings to kites
or red balloons

We soar through this house, my brother and I
holding hands to keep from falling
as the stairs crumble and tilt like sculpted sand
and the upper floors sag and bow, boards broken, rugs soft
as a tablecloth covering a hole in wet cardboard:
say the magic word,
pull the rug,
we all fall down

Up here it is always the last visit:
Grandpa talks about his birds, shows us
beaks and feathers, tiny blue wings
under glass up here where the morning air
is dim with dust, while Grandma's
jewelry chests hold secrets:
she opens them slyly to let speaking stories slip free:
the feathers she saved from her Blackfoot great-grandfather;
the feathers our grandpa gave for her bridal veil;
the reason turquoise, the sky-stone,
has always been her favorite

There's not much we can do
from this far away:
nothing my brother and I
can take home from this treasure-filled attic
where dust coats boxes of broken cars and little flags,
lost wooden men from long-gone games,
the salvaged remnants of dreams shared by

a little boy and his grandpa

All the embroidered mottoes, the dollhouses, teacups,
little porcelain birds, cabinets stuffed with yellowed pages,
the handwriting still bold and strong with youth--
no way to tell what's important,
except we know it all is:
we can't even save the stories of Great-Aunt Ida,
or Grandma's high school graduation
and debut spring

When we wake up, only their smiles
and the memory of siblings and cousins fighting over dusty toys
will remain as we groan and creak up from our perch
in the two magic reclining chairs
we made out of salvage from the old studio couch on which Grandpa
gave our fictional selves
magic carpet rides

The Time Traveler's Weekend
Adele Gardner

I. The Time Traveler Embarks
I love the way you step back in time
without a backward glance,
as easy as stepping on a plane,
bags all packed, travel guides memorized, this foreign land
mapped out in your mind, familiar.
Cross the line, and you're
not a twenty-first-century man at all,
but something quite different:
knowing how they thought and lived then
becomes simply thinking and living, these "props"
your rightful clothes and food.
For the duration, you believe
your wife actually stitched these homespun clothes,
baked your bread from scratch in a stone oven.
Saying farewell to me, you speak the truth:
"I'm off to the wars to strike a blow for freedom."
I've seen your souvenirs—coins blackened with age and use,
the tattered flag you nearly died defending,
the scar from the stomach wound you would have died from,
had you stayed in that colonial age.
Instead, in my present, I rush you to the emergency room,
still in your colonial clothes. From your coat pocket

you press a letter into my hand, stained with your own blood,
smeared by the dirt of centuries.
The doctors stitch you up, neat as you strike your tent.
You're well, at home, except
for the frost still biting a corner of your heart
from all the friends you lost at Valley Forge.

II. The Time Traveler Returns

You don't kick back on weekends: you kick off,
trading sneakers for straight-last shoes,
strapping on bedroll, rifle, cooking pan,
grabbing your tent and poles to vault into the past.
It's not that things were easier. You're glad to come home,
cheerfully praising pure water, vaccines, toilets—
at least for the first twenty-four hours.
You swear you wouldn't want to live there.
Things were terrible for slaves, the first nations, women, the poor.
Even the rich died "old" at half our span. Women were sacrificed
on the altar of birthing beds, worn down after seventeen trials,
the proliferation of babies essential because so few survived.
Maybe the air was cleaner high above, but here below
the cities reeked of coal, wood fires, excrement;
and swamp air bred yellow fever in close, stifled rooms.
Geography killed: those colorful, hand-drawn maps don't show
crushing winters and too-short springs, scant harvests,
treks across trackless forests and snowy mountains,
parched, lost, eating our own kind.
Yet present life wearies you: lawyers, FBI, layoffs, recession,
pollution, extinction, starvation, epidemics, global warming.
You drag through the week, worrying
that there's no future for anyone here, at the end of our planet.
We don't know what's next, but most of it looks bad. At best,
we might return to backyard gardens and bicycles, walk to our jobs,
build things with our own hands—while the luxuries you return for
            vanish
under the crush of surviving babies.
Whatever the hardships, the endless toil, the suffering,
the future was better there--because we had one.
We had the luxury of belief in our own immortality—
that inheritors would guard the human story;
that the human race would carry on.
So you grow restless when the intervals stretch between trips, elongating
till they snap you back. You salute goodbye in one ecstatic wave.
Your absence lengthens. You come back for work Mondays,
then Tuesdays. I call in for you when I wake up alone.
You can return at any time you want, and yet
you're skipping days, weeks. You spend your vacation there,

then work out a flex plan, avoiding the present by working
straight through to the moment you'll leave again.
Soon it will be leave without pay, months, whole years.
There's more gray at your temples each time I see you.
Will you be kind and scatter days through my life like a blessing?
When you're here, you're like a ghost already.
I know each time you return might be the last.
You might decide to stay in the past.
In the future, I might be dead.
But I clutch hope like the presents you bring home,
praying with all my might that I don't know the future:
that humans will smarten up in time to salvage something—
that the next time you come back,
you'll take me with you.

The Still Point of the Turning World

Adrienne J. Odasso

1. Cather's Run

I thought it was the stream
where the crayfish hid, where the wind
once knocked me clean in. So, I swam
for the bank by way of the deep
and dived instead. The trout teem
in this darkness divisible: my arms
cut a wide, white arc in the shallows
and then down like an arrow,
but bent. I touched rocks six feet under
where my feet slid on algae. Death came
to count the ticking of my fast-held breath.
Shivering, dragged to the surface, I went.

2. Harvard Square

It doesn't work like that, she said.

One does not blink out and rekindle, must not
dare to return to haunt the living. *Well, I dare*,
I said, and the sterling spoon there, tyre-bent and slivered,

agreed. Some ancient polarity, the universe's heart

hangs on a thread. I bought my fare here, silver, too,
and hung it from a chain. I will not show it to the sun,
nor name it before the living. The prow of this ship

veers star-ward true as the traffic light turns green.

3. Rievaulx Abbey

My breath returned that day
in the rain, up the rise
to where my eyes
fell on the walls. I cried
as if I'd found some fabled answer,
feral comfort
in the lichens' loving scrape.

A chaser of pillars with stories
is what I became:

no hallowed ruin thereafter
was spared my embrace.

4. St. James's Park

Stay with me a while, he says.

And the water rises to the pavement, lifts
my coat, forms the wildest of wings. Sifts
the sand from my skull and gifts me
with snail-shells for teeth. I am

the duck-dive, the bird-cry, the breeze
through the bridges and leaves. I am silence
in the man's startled eyes as I pass by the table
where he's sat. Spark recognition. *I'm your ghost,*
I want to say, *and you're mine, but next time —*

Next time won't be so simple:
I'll sink and not rise.

The eyes beneath which you shiver
will not be mine.

Asteres Planetai

Amal El-Mohtar

> *Ancient Greek astronomers coined the term asteres planetai ( ), or "wandering
> stars", for celestial bodies which appeared to move across the sky.*

I.

I used to think I was a star.

I used to think
I am only visible at night.

I used to think

that when the world's face turned from the sun,
blinking narrow eyes at an emptied sky,
there would I be, pulsing
with my own light.

But I am not a star.

II.

My depths and surfaces are scored
with meteoric phrases, burning on entry,
blazing, unexpected.

It's only a phase.
Disgusting.
Unnatural.
Not while you're under my roof.

These grooves, these lakes, these hills and valleys
wander with me,
warp my weight,
tilt my axis by small degrees
that make all the difference.

In these ways, too,
I am not a star.
When the sun's beams ebb from the sky
like tidal fingers, I shine—
but still
I am not a star.

III.

Stars, like the sun,
know their place.

Because they can trace
with beautiful precision
their distance from each other,
they demand to know
their distance from me.

I shake my head,
behold my shining feet.
I have no fixed abode.
I make my home of motion—
I cannot stand still.
And my light—

You are a star.
You are like us.

Stay with us in the dark.
Everyone will see you for what you are.

I love the dark.
But if I were to stand still in the dark
and look like a star,
I would only be half myself,
and though I yearn for them with my core
and my gravity,
and I am full, so full, of heat,
I am not a star.

IV.

I do not fall like stars do.
Stars fall out of place, and mourn the loss—I
fall *in* to place.
When the falling has me, I
twist my body into orbit,
make a sun of my love,
feel my face become bright with theirs.

If I love in the dark, I seem a star.
If I love in the day, I do not.

A sun, after all,
is a star
who has chosen never to be seen in the dark.

V.

At noon I look
like what the world calls a woman.

I wander from the sky
on to roads warm with day,
see my arms brown with it.

By day I meet a creature
patient as the morning, and as kind,
with sun-sky eyes,
a gentle mouth.

I fall.

We wander graveyards, seashores,
talk of kings and cormorants,
hold each other's hands.

I tell my sun-bright creature
that in the dark, I glow.

I shine.

But you are not in the dark, observes my creature.

I speak of the beauty of the stars,
of my longing to wander always near them,
of how, though I am not a star,
I gleam like them
in the dark.

You do not gleam with me, says my creature.

I do. I do.
But you eclipse me.
You are so bright—
and you live within the day—
and you know nothing of the dark—
if I stay with you,
encircle you,
if I stay fallen in this place with you,
I will never be seen in the dark again,
never shine with stars again. *Just a phase,*
as if the moon did not have more than a face,
as if to orbit is to stand still—
you're fixed now
and
you faked it
and
your light was our reflection.

My creature's hands encircle my face,
shade it from the sun,
coax a shining from it:

I am not afraid of the dark.

VI.
I used to think I was a star.

I used to think
I am only visible at night.

But, strange to find—
there are times in-between,
lights by which I can be seen.
I learn new words to tell my hours:
dusk and *dawn* and *twi* and *gloam,*
wander through them holding hands,
burning to be known.

Into Flight

Andrew Robert Sutton

It was just one zero too many
one gadget too much.
The books gave up and,
in a flurry, took flight.

How? Scientists couldn't say.
Where to? Only the mystic,
crystal-toting, tarot-reading
lunatic fringe would even conjecture.

Most kids didn't even notice,
cocooned in their networks
of empty streams of bits and bytes.
That in itself might account for the Why.

The little ones took to wing first—
homilies and pocket Bibles.
They darted away quietly
between one glance and the next.

Then, the paperbacks,
Bradbury's stuff leading the way,
winging off to Mars, pulps in tow.
A few thought this a wonder.

Soon though, the Oxford dictionary,
Norton's anthology, and Shakespeare
(Riverside editions) were aloft.
Then came the law books. Lord! The law books.

That's when it became impossible
not to notice. Only then did anyone care—
when it was too much,
when it was too inconvenient

They interfered with things—
the beautiful, fluttering books.
They brought air traffic to a standstill,
and that was just for starters.

They frightened pets and startled drivers.
They smashed into windows
and had a predilection for power lines
that could very nearly be called a vendetta.

Some of the volumes, in their vigor,
shed pages, showered the world
with poetry and cliffhangers
and snippets of wonder.

Office districts were soon buried
in white like Narnia in perpetual winter.
After a few damps nights, entire city blocks
were entombed in papier mâché.

Antique districts swirled into yellowed autumns,
Washington transformed into a Hitchcockian hell
with tax-code books circling slowly overhead
like buzzards awaiting prey.

Some lonely readers thought to lure
their loved ones home. Other readers plotted
to recapture them by trickery—
their methods as varied as their genre.

Poetry lovers were seen sprinting
through meadows with butterfly nets,
or canary cages baited with binder's glue,
singing line and verse.

Mystery fans sleuthed while suspense
fans waited on tenterhooks. Horror
fans gathered to scribe ISBN numbers
into hearts of pentagrams, elaborately, in red.

Baristas advised wafting cappuccino vapors
out the windows while lawyers filed injunctions
against authors, ordering them to cease
their trickery or face consequences.

Some readers even tried to signal them
with book lights from the rooftops.
Once, for a single night, the world lit up
like a great ocean reflecting the night stars.

But, as difficult as they were to pen, words
were ten times more elusive on the wing.
Try as readers might, the books wouldn't listen
to reason and they couldn't be caught.

Certain people had the temerity to shoot
at them, drunk and cocksure,
thinking the entire thing some grand sport.
That proved to be unwise.

Hemingway, Twain, and, even Dickens
wouldn't stand for such impudence,
and the men with guns
suddenly couldn't run fast enough.

It was clear the books wouldn't come down.
Citizens demanded solutions.
Officials all over the world took steps—
convened in capitols, passed resolutions.

They evicted molly-coddling librarians,
chained shut the library doors
boarded up the busted windows.
Posted guards.

Briefly, it was poetic.
All the books fluttering
like exotic butterflies in gardens
or snowflakes in enormous globes.

The books didn't tire, though,
and soon the libraries, too, were aloft,
hovering like giant zeppelins, plunging
cities, then the states, into twilight.

And then one night, just like that
without any ceremony or fanfare,
they left the world—ascending—
never to return.

Yes, the text was still there:
digitized, sanitized, organized.
But it wasn't the same,
and it wasn't long before people knew it.

Like salt without savor,
like flowers without scent,
the text was without soul
and offered nothing to their readers.

There were no sanctuaries of silence,
no temples of free thought.
There was only a gaping void
where no one had expected one—

the world had become a darker place.
Soon, men fashioned paper wings
scribed them with wild tales,
their eyes fixed heavenward.

Thirteen Ways of Looking At and Through Hashish

After Clark Ashton Smith and Wallace Stevens

Bruce Boston

The Art

Women Smoking Hashish, 1887,
by Italian Pointillist/Symbolist
Gaetano Previati, 1852–1920,
is a drab and moralistic
interior landscape,
executed in shades
of dull brown
grained and splashed
by pale yellow,
a bit like the shade
of fine Moroccan hash.

Four women slouch
on chairs and a couch,
dressed heavily
in the long layered
style of the era,
heads thrown back
in stuporous enchantment,
eyes closed
beneath a low-ceilinged room.

Here is a vision
opaque as the canvas
on which it is painted.

At the rear of the room,
through windows stained
by indelible smoke,
the strained light
fails to illuminate
the scene beyond.

The women look
as if they could
never stir again
and remain satisfied
unto death.

In all of this
depressing tableau,
there is no hint

of the colors
that obsess their minds,
nor the visions
that now consume
their lives.

The Rush

you know   man
this is just the way
it comes on for me

probably different
for everyone

when I smoke hash
you know   that first rush
it comes on like
no other drug

you ever been to
one of those classical concerts
with the big orchestras

well   hash
is like that orchestra
from one of those concerts
tuning up in the orchestra pit

that's how it comes on
when I smoke it
I like to call it
the tuning fork of hash

man   it's strange
and kind of awesome
the way it comes on at first

all the instruments making
different noises that
have nothing to do with
one another

like you can feel
the different parts
of your brain
tuning up
for the high like that

flaring up a little at a time

and getting
kind of all synchronized
and ready take off
together

and then gradually
one by one
they die down
to a steady glow
and there is a moment
or two of silence

no   almost silence

and you know—
to continue this riff
—maybe there is
a cough from the audience
the rustle of people
shifting in their chairs—
or maybe it's like
a rifling of pages
through your mind
too fast to read
and then it starts
hits you all at once
like a brush fire

takes the lid off
the top of your head
like some Crumb cartoon

and you are eight miles high
and all kinds of things
coming rushing in

and you can become
just about anything
and be anywhere
you want to be

The Flight

I am the rider
of the silken beast
of passionate hallucination.
I am the beast itself.

I grasp my mane
over twenty snowy mountains

and twenty flaming rivers.

I am the emperor
of red imagination
and ice cream dreams.

I am the black bird
whose shadow wing
sweeps the moon
in its flickering embrace,

the midnight vision
that slyly haunts
your shallow afternoons,

a wild storm of shades
that returns with evening,
nourished and aroused.

I am the fierce raptor
whose swan song
you have yet to hear.

The Victim

Assaulted by chords
Of apocalyptic thunder
Gliding forth from
The deepest pits
Of some Stygian hell,
Chords of fey emancipation
And wild enslavements,
Enabled by demons
Conversing in a humid
Garbled gutter tongue
As they debate my fate,
I am of a single mind
Of manifold illusions,
A tree whose branches
Never stop sprouting
Leaves and flowers
In networks interlacing,
Immersed in a morphing world
Of glyphs and ruins,
And amaranthine terrains,
Adrift in rich persecutions
And megalomanias,
I am crowned The King
Of My Own Distorted Dreams.

Passage of the Beast

I rush down dark tunnels with filthy water slogging
about my boots, the jagged cave walls about me

embedded with a luminous aromatic fungi casting
a pale odiferous light that sparks diamond flecks

and wafts the aroma of burnt cinnamon and sugar,
an ominous ocher light that ripples and undulates

with amorphous and anthropomorphic shapes.
Baroque encrustations accelerate toward me,

lost impresa embossed with intaglios like brands.
The archaeological debris of a thousand empires

coagulates in the corridors of my mind and I
embrace the hollow rites of ritual slaughter,

make pacts with demons of my shattered soul.
I fashion barbarian homunculi warriors who

writhe forth from the dark soil at my bidding.
I plunder riches from the hoards of my enemies.

I ride the helpless virgins like Khan or Attila,
seizing mates from the conquered hordes.

Once I emerge on the surface of the earth
the world is transformed to my bidding.

A glass carriage iridescent with northern lights
appears before me, its lucent seats cushioned

with extravagant pillows of liquid burgundy.
I embark on a journey that seems without end,

sailing over seascapes, landscapes, cityscapes.
Now it is dawn across this world of my making.

I hear black birds cawing the chorus of the hunt.
I hear their strident song and I see their shadows

swift against the sky and on the slanted streets.
I listen as they sing the dark legend of my life.

The Hashshashin

In the nanosecond
left to him
and his life,

as the bomb detonated,
he realized there
would be no paradise.
no virgins, no smoke.

The Chemistry

let me tell you
about this hash
that you are going
to want to buy
from me

ever heard of trichomes?
that's where the action is

they're these glandular hairs
that stick up from the buds
and flowers of the female
Cannabis sativa plant

that's where the THC
the tetrahydrocannabinol
is most concentrated
and will take you
wherever you
want to go

cause you got these
cannabinoid receptors
located on neurons
scattered throughout
your brain and body
(just sitting there
ready and waiting
to get turned on)

and once the THC
binds with those receptors
your synapses start clicking
like a chain reaction
and that's when you
really begin to fly

now most hash
it's got maybe
thirty forty percent
trichomes mixed
in with a bunch

of leaves and flowers

but this hash
that you're going
to want to buy
from me
is Moroccan hash
the very best
and it's got sixty
percent guaranteed

you take one or two
hits and it's all
you're going to
ever need to fly
wherever you
want to go

the only question is
how much do you
want to buy?

The Gourmand

She ate furry trichomes
and fly agaric
from the cups
of flamboyant mushrooms.

She devoured rubies
of the finest persuasion
and emeralds
from the hearts of lizards.

She swallowed
diamonds drenched
in the aqua vitae
of extraterrestrial streams,

consumed spatulate
leaves of unknown origin
and incredible effect.
She graced the

tasteless crackers of the Host
with truffles and brie,
with fungal infestations
bred in the cellars

of decadent aristocrats,

washed them down with
nectar of absinthe
and sun-stroked afternoons.

She drowned diligently
in the inimitable
pleasures of bizarre taste
and visionary extravaganza.

The Synesthesia

Shadow lines of night
close on the horizon,
slicing the last sounds of light
to strips so thin
they are ultrasonic,

like finely hammered
gold leaf
pressed
to the thickness of a single atom,
so thin they are transparent
to the inner ear
in the yellow lamps of dusk,

so thin you
can almost hear
their translucent shades,
taste their fragrance
on the tines of tomorrow.

The Flight of Language

I experience enchantments
of mythic proportions.
I am the owl and the raven,

the kingfisher, the heron,
the eagle and the hawk.
All birds of prey

forever in flight
or about to take flight,
all birds black in silhouette

against a harsh horizon,
diverse hybrids
of the same inky strain.

I explode to fractal feathers

beneath a semiotic sky
engraved with cloud runes

and clouds glyphs
in a language arcane
and illuminating.

As if words were riven
by endless dichotomies,
an ongoing dialectic,

each thought entrenched
and bastioned by others,
beleaguered by innuendo

and extended hyperbole,
lodged as a riddle
in a complex puzzle box,

the aged grain of its wood
darkened and polished
through the centuries

by hands that have
tried to unravel
its wiredrawn intricacy,

by minds that have
tried to unhinge
the sky.

The History

let me tell you
when you eat hash
when you smoke hash
you become part
of a grand tradition
of enhanced consciousness
and individual expression
stretching back centuries

thousands of years ago
let's say   ten or so
this cat somewhere
in the Himalayas
gets real hungry

no food anywhere
so he decides to eat some

leaves and flowers
off this weed growing
just about everywhere

now   they don't do
much for his hunger
but they do a lot
of things for his head
so he shares them
with his friends
now   time trip with me
for a minute or two
several thousand years
to be exact

the word has spread
in every direction
and so has the trade
all round Asia
east to China
south to India

it's not called a weed
anymore but sacred grass,
bhang, bhangi, keef, charas

Shiva   that Indian avatar
is dubbed the Lord of Bhang

meanwhile   this other cat
(and who knows
maybe he's a descendant
of that first cat?)
starts fooling around
until he finds the best
parts of sacred grass
and from these
he conjures
the first hashish

and pretty soon all
those ancient cats
are smoking it
eating it   smoking it

Scythians, Persians
Siberians, Samaritans,
Hiptherians, Dylusians,
you name

some ancient folk
from thereabouts
and you can bet
some of them
were getting high

now   stay with me here
jumping a few more years
and getting specific
about the time of Jesus
the first stash boxes
start showing up
coincidence?

900–1000
hashish spreads swiftly
through all of Arabia
and creeps into Europe
on a shady afternoon

1378
the Emir of the Ottoman Empire
issues a ban against hashish
throughout his kingdom
yeah   even back then
they were shooting
down the dreamers

mid-16th century
Arabian poet Mohammad Foruli
writes a long allegorical poem
about a battle between
hashish and wine
neither wins

1798
after conquering Egypt
Napoleon bans
the use of hash there
though his troops
carry it home

45 years later
le Club des hachichins
is founded
by the literati of France
(Dumas, Baudelaire,
Gautier, Nerval)
and opens in Paris,

devoted mainly
to the eating of hash
in hash-eating company

1887
Italian artist
Gaetano Previati
paints and exhibits
Women Smoking Hashish
a dire and desolate
interior landscape

1920
American author
Clark Ashton Smith
pens an epic poem
on eating hashish
that paints in words
what Gaetano failed
to paint on his canvas

1920–1940
Greece and China
ban hash smoking
while its cultivation
and use flourish in India
Bangladesh is known
as the Capital of Bhang

1980
Morocco becomes
the world's major
producer of hashish

1995
hashish is
sold openly
in Amsterdam
coffeehouses

today
this very instant

now I'm part
of this history
the trade and tradition
the expression
and I'm passing
it on to you

would you like a toke?

The Art Revisited

It was snowing dark smoke
and it was going to snow
dark smoke.

It was snowing
the story of tomorrow
and it was going to snow

the story of tomorrow.
It was going to snow
for a good time to come.

Falling steadily
and finding its way
into lives scattered

throughout the globe.
With black birds gliding
on the feverish winds

of that storm.
And the canvas
darker and more

detailed with age
than any artist
could fashion.

The Afterglow

Tendrils of illumination
Cling to my thoughts,
Trailing in my wake,
Puzzling to those
Whose paths I cross,
Those ever immersed
In the dull endurance
Of their daily tasks,
Without illusions,
Without perception
Of what lies beyond
The stolid borders
Of the everyday,
Insensate and
Unable to travel
In the domains

Of space and time
And consciousness.

The Last Crone on the Moon
C.S.E. Cooney

1.

At daybreak she espies them
twisting through the curls
sneakily they glint, the vanguard
just a few threads yet
tangle-snaked and
gray

she auditions similes against mortality:
hair like rain, like winter rivers, like
quicksilver, spiderweb, wolfpelt
(fails, feels instantly endangered
her mouth a quarter quavering
mostly wry)

later, they multiply
strand by strand
miles on the road
deadlines, payload
lean times, deathblows
friends made, faded, more and more
she braids gray with gold

2.

"room enough for all gods' children on the moon!
step right up, sit down, lean back — aaaand freeze!
all the rest'll keep, so here's a little somethin-somethin to
help you sleep; sweethearts, sleep
a hundred years (give or take), and we'll
wake you with a smootheroo, and we'll
have the stuff by then to make you
young and beautiful again"

up and out they go
smooth-browed, serene and clean
unbreathing
whole generations
by the rocketshipful

she watches

the world empties.

3.

when the last is decades gone
in a fastness of iron-and-diamond caskets
tended by tender robots
she coils her hair into a coronet, takes her
cane by the carving of the crow's head
walks briskly but with stiff steps to the kiosk
where the android with the ticktock heart
reads her retinas and greets her by name

"just once," she says, "I want to see
my shadow cast by earthlight."

"that I can do," smiles the android (ticktock)
"but the flight itself might murder you
you ain't no spring chicken, miss daisy
more of a Methuselah, I'm thinkin'
maybe a Tithonus, sort of shrunk and sunken
shriveled like a cricket
however spry."

"all too true, my gearish dear — I agree with you!
yet here I stand
weatherworn
worm-eaten as I am
applying for the post
of last crone on the moon

see,
when at last tomorrow's children awaken
on that barren rock, in that vacuum vastness
shaking in the dark and cold
I reckon they'll be wanting something old
to cling to."

Mouse Koan

Catherynne M. Valente

I.

In the beginning of everything
I mean the real beginning
the only show in town
was a super-condensed blue-luminous ball
of everything

that would ever be
including your mother
and the 1984 Olympics in Los Angeles
and the heat-death of prime time television
            a pink-white spangle-froth
of deconstructed stars
burst
into the eight million gods of this world.
Some of them were social creatures
some misanthropes, hiding out in the asteroid belt
turning up their ion-trails at those sell-outs trying to teach
the dinosaurs about ritual practice
and the importance of regular hecatombs. It was
a lot like high school. The popular kids figured out the game
right away. Sun gods like football players firing glory-cannons
downfield
bookish virgin moon-nerds
angry punkbrat storm gods shoving sacrificial
gentle bodied compassion-niks
into folkloric lockers. But one
a late bloomer, draft dodger
in Ragnarok, that mess with the Titans,
both Armageddons,
        started showing up around 1928. Your basic
trickster template
                genderless
                primary colors
                making music out of goat bellies
                                cow udders
                                ram horns
            squeezing cock ribs like bellows.
It drew over its face
the caul of a vermin animal,
all black circles and disruption. Flickering
silver and dark
it did not yet talk
it did not yet know its nature.
Gods
have problems with identity, too. No better
than us
they have midlife crises
run out
drive a brand new hot red myth cycle
get a few mortals pregnant with
half-human monster-devas who
grow up to be game show hosts
ask themselves in the long terrible confusion

of their personal centuries
who am I, really?
what does any of it mean?
I'm so afraid
someday everyone will see
that I'm just an impostor
a fake among all the real
and gorgeous godheads.
                    The trickster god of silent films
knew of itself only:
I am a mouse.
I love nothing.
I wish to break
everything.
                    It did not even know
what it was god of
what piece of that endlessly exploding
heating and cooling and shuddering and scattering cosmos
it could move.
                    But that is no obstacle
to hagiography.
                    Always in motion
                    plane/steamboat/galloping horse
even magic cannot stop its need
to stomp and snap
to unzip order:
                    if you work a dayjob
                              wizard
                              boat captain
                              orchestra man
beware.

                    A priesthood called it down
like a moon
men with beards
men with money.
                    It wanted not love
nor the dreamsizzle of their ambition
but to know itself.
                    Tell me who I am, it said.
And they made icons of it in black and white
then oxblood and mustard and gloves
like the paws of some bigger beast.
They gave it a voice
                    falsetto and terrible
though the old school gods know the value
of silence.
                    They gave it a consort

like it but not
it.
     A mirror-creature in a red dress forever
out of reach
as impenetrable and unpenetrating
as itself.
     And for awhile
the mouse-god ran loose
eating
     box office
     celluloid
     copyright law
     human hearts
and called it good.

II.

If you play Fantasia backwards
you can hear the mantra of the mouse-god sounding.

     Hiya, kids!
Let me tell you something true:
    the future
    is plastics
the future
is me.
     I am the all-dancing thousand-eared unembodied god of
Tomorrowland.
And only in that distant
Space Mountain Age of glittering electro-synthetic perfection
will I become fully myself, fully
apotheosed, for only then
will you be so tired of my laughing iconographic infinitely fertile and reproducing
perpetual smile-rictus
my red trousers that battle Communism
my PG-rated hidden and therefore monstrous genitalia
my bawdy lucre-yellow shoes
so deaf to my jokes
your souls hardened like arteries
that I can rest.
     Contrary to what you may have heard
it is possible
to sate a trickster.
     It only takes the whole world.
   But look,
don't worry about it. That's not what I'm about
anymore. Everybody
grows up.

Everybody
grows clarity,
which is another name
for the tumor that kills you.
　　　　I finally
figured it out.
You don't know what it's like
　　　　to be a god without a name tag.
HELLO MY NAME IS
　　　　nothing. What? God of corporate ninja daemonic fuckery?
That's not me. That's not
the theme song
I came out of the void beyond Jupiter
to dance to.
　　　　The truth is
I'm here to rescue you.

　　　　The present and the future are a dog
racing a duck. Right now
you think happiness
is an industrial revolution that lasts forever.
Brings to its own altar
the Chicken of Tomorrow
breasts heavy with saline
　　　　　　　margarine
　　　　　　　dehydrated ice cream
　　　　　　　freeze-dried coffee crystals
Right now, monoculture
feels soft and good and right
as Minnie in the dark.
　　　　　It's 1940.
　　　　　You're not ready yet.
　　　　　You can't know.
Someday
everything runs down.
Someday
entropy unravels the very best of us.
Someday
all copyright runs out.
　　　　　In that impossible futurological post-trickster space
I will survive
I will become my utter self
　　　　　and this is it:
I am the god
of the secret world-on-fire
that the corporate all-seeing eye
cannot see.
I am the song of perfect kitsch

endless human mousefire
burning toward mystery
                    I am ridiculous
                    and unlovely
                    I am plastic
                    and mass-produced
I am the tiny threaded needle
of unaltered primordial unlawful beauty-after-horror
                    of everything that is left of you
                    glittering glorified
                    when the Company Man
                    has used you up
                    to build the Company Town.
Hey.
they used me, too.
I thought we were just having fun. Put me in the movies, mistah!
The flickies! The CINEMA.
The 20s were one long champagne binge.

          I used to be
a goggling plague mouse shrieking deadstar spaceheart
          now I'm a shitty
          fire retardant polyurethane
          keychain.
Hey there. Hi there. Ho there.
What I am the god of
is the fleck of infinite timeless
hilarious
nuclear inferno soul
that can't be trademarked
patented bound up in international courts
the untraded future.
                    That's why
                    my priests
                    can never let me go
                    screaming black-eared chaotic red-assed jetmouse
                    into the collective unconscious Jungian unlost Eden
                    called by the mystic name of public domain
                    The shit I would kick up there
                    if I were free!
I tricked them good. I made them
put my face on the moon.
I made them take me everywhere
their mouse on the inside
I made them so fertile
they gave birth to a billion of me.
                    Anything that common
will become invisible.

And in that great plasticene Epcotfutureworld
you will have no trouble finding me.
Hey.
You're gonna get hurt. Nothing
I can do.
Lead paint grey flannel suits toxic runoff
monoculture like a millstone
fairy tales turned into calorie-free candy
you don't even know
what corporate downsizing is yet.
And what I got
isn't really much
What I got
is a keychain
What I got
is the pure lotuslove
of seeing the first lightspray of detonated creation
even in the busted-up world they sell you.
Seeing in me
as tired and overworked
as old gum
the unbearable passionmouse of infinite stupid trashcamp joy
and hewing to that.
It's the riddle of me, baby. I am
everywhere   exploited   exhibited   exhausted
and I am still holy.
It doesn't matter
what they do to you.
Make you a permanent joke
sell your heart off piece by piece
robber princes
ruin everything
it's what they do
like a baby cries.
Look at my opposite number.
It was never coyote versus
roadrunner.
It was both
against Acme
mail order daemon of death.
Stick with me. Someday
we'll bundle it all up again
the big blue-luminous ball of everything
your father
the Tunguska event
the ultimate star-spangled obliteration of all empires.
I will hold everything tawdry
in my gloved four-fingered hand

and hold it high
                 high
                 high.
It's 1940. What you don't know
is going to break you.   Listen to the Greek chorus
of my Kids
lining up toward the long downward slide of the century
like sacrifices.
                        Their song comes backward and upside down
                        from the unguessable extropy
                        of that strangesad orgiastic corporate electrical parade
                        of a future
                        Listen to it.
                        The sound of my name
                        the letters forty feet high.
See ya
see ya
see ya real soon.

What the Dragon Said: A Love Story
Catherynne M. Valente

So this guy walks into a dragon's lair
    and he says
why the long tale?
        HAR HAR BUDDY
says the dragon
        FUCK YOU.

The dragon's a classic
the '57 Chevy of existential chthonic threats
take in those Christmas colors, those
impervious green scales, sticky candy-red firebreath,
comes standard with a heap of rubylust
goldhuddled treasure.
        Go ahead.
        Kick the tires, boy.
        See how she rides.

Sit down, kid, says the dragon. Diamonds
roll off her back like dandruff.

Oh, you'd rather be called a paladin?
I'd rather be a unicorn.
        Always thought that
was the better gig. Everyone thinks
you're innocent. Everyone calls you

pure. And the girls aren't afraid
they come right up with their little hands out
for you to sniff
like you're a puppy
and they're gonna take you home.
They let you put your head right
in their laps.
            But nobody on this earth
ever got what they wanted. Now

I know what you came for. You want
my body. To hang it up on a nail
over your fireplace. Say to some milk-and-rosewater chica
who lays her head in your lap
look how much it takes
to make me feel like a man.
            We're in the dark now, you and me. This is primal
shit right here. Grendel, Smaug, St. George. You've been
called up. This is the big game. You don't have
to make stupid puns. Flash your feathers
like your monkey bravado
can impress. I saw a T-Rex fight a comet
and lose. You've
got nothing I want.

Here's something I bet you don't know:
            every time someone writes a story about a dragon
a real dragon dies.
            Something about seeing
and being seen
            something about mirrors
that old tune about how a photograph
can take your whole soul. At the end
of this poem
            I'm going to go out like electricity
in an ice storm. I've made peace with it.
            That last blockbuster took out a whole family
            of Bhutan thunder dragons
living in Latvia
the fumes of their cleargas hoard
hanging on their beards like blue ghosts.

A dragon's gotta get zen
            with ephemerality.

You want to cut me up? Chickenscratch my leather
with butcher's chalk:
cutlets, tenderloin, ribs for the company barbecue,

chuck, chops, brisket, roast.
       I dig it, I do.
I want to eat everything, too.

When I look at the world
      I see a table.
All those fancy houses, people with degrees, horses and whales,
bankers and Buddha statues
the Pope, astronauts, panda bears and yes, paladins
      if you let me swallow you whole
      I'll call you whatever you want.
Look at it all: waitresses and ice caps and submarines down
at the bottom of the heavy lightless saltdark of the sea
      Don't they know they'd be safer
      inside me?

I could be big for them
      I could hold them all
My belly could be a city
      where everyone was so loved
they wouldn't need jobs. I could be
the hyperreal
post-scarcity dragonhearted singularity.
      I could eat them
      and feed them
      and eat them
      and feed them.

This is why I don't get to be a unicorn.
Those ponies have clotted cream and Chanel No. 5 for blood
and they don't burn up like comets
with love that tastes like starving to death.
      And you, with your standup comedy knightliness,
covering Beowulf's greatest hits on your tin kazoo,
you can't begin to think through
      what it takes to fill up a body like this.
It takes everything pretty
and everything true
      and you stick yourself in a cave because
your want is bigger than you.

I just want to be
the size of a galaxy
so I can eat all the stars and gas giants
without them noticing
and getting upset.
Is that so bad?
      Isn't that

what love looks like?
        Isn't that
what you want, too?

I'll make you a deal.
    Come close up
stand on my emeraldheart, my sapphireself
the goldpile of my body
    Close enough to smell
everything you'll never be.

Don't finish the poem. Not for nothing
is it a snake
that eats her tail
and means eternity. What's a few verses worth
anyway? Everyone knows
poetry doesn't sell. Don't you ever feel
like you're just
a story someone is telling
about someone like you?
            I get that. I get you. You and me
we could fit
inside each other. It's not nihilism
if there's really no point to anything.

I have a secret
down in the deep of my dark.
All those other kids who wanted me
to call them paladins,
warriors, saints, whose swords had names,
whose bodies were perfect
as moonlight
    they've set up a township near my liver
had babies with the maidens they didn't save
    invented electric lightbulbs
    thought up new holidays.
            You can have my body
            just like you wanted.
Or you can keep on fighting dragons
writing dragons
fighting dragons
re-staging that same old Cretaceous deathmatch
you mammals
always win.
            But hey, hush, come on.
Quit now.
You'll never fix
that line.

I have a forgiveness in me
the size of eons
and if a dragon's body is big enough
it just looks like the world.

Did you know
the earth used to have two moons?

Tit Tot

Catt Kingsgrave

I'll have this known at the start—I gave that girl my name.
Oh yes, and roll your eyes, but truly;
Nimmy nimmy nott?
Think ye the Sidhe, who've sung the ages down,
Charmed queens, nuns and virgins to summerhill maying,
Led knights and kings in circles lifetimes long,
Coaxed battlements from rosebriars, truth from false men's tongues,
And honeyed gold from bristling flax can rhyme no better?

Know this, Mayfly; my kind are not as yours
For deceive we may, and without regret,
But never do we lie.
It is a point of fighting pride with us, you see,
And we have shed our ageless blood like pearls in black loam
For merely the shadow
Of untruth between great hills.
Now roll your eyes and call me liar again?
Ah, no.
And wisely done.

I gave my name away that day,
And too, the bargain I'd come to regret,
Glib-lipped and cocksure; lured in by her honeysuckle tears
Pearl pale and sweet with despair in her tiny dungeon boudoir.
I had wished so to taste of them, and dip
My tongue into the wellspring of her mortal heart.
To know her,
From suspicion to sorrow,
Hope to horror,
Delight to despair and back again.
Well, that much I did in one moon's time, I warrant,
But she did not come to love me.

Oh, perhaps a little at first, with gleaming gold piled up
To ward her from the headsman's steel.
She did weep for me then, a little, and her grateful tears

Were silk and diamond and lily petals in the dawning ...
But though I had bought her a day with my night's toil
She took three tries at me straight away.
And so I knew it was not love.
Not John. Not Hob. Not Nicodemos.
And not Love.

Not just yet, perhaps, but only let her see
Her Prince's eyes agleam upon her morning ransom;
Adoring avarice, pretty words and breakfast
And a nice bed for the day,
And how
He spared but one hand to lead her away,
The other busy with her skeins of gold.
My gold. My courting gift. Oh yes,
Just let my girl be led back below when nightfall came,
Locked in, her sentence just the same, and
Faithful only me, I come—
Come once again to save her.
Surely she would learn to love me then.
But no.
Not Harald. Not Timothy. Not Abraxas.

"Woman, I will take you away,"
I told her upon another night, for I'd a place in mind
Where girls' bright hours waste not away
In airless dungeon rooms, and their evenings sing
With fireflies and briar wine, not wheels and spindling greed
And if they live but briefly to our ageless span?
Oh but their days are bright.
Her eyes lit to my promise by grudging candle's glow,
Welled tears more fine than cats' dreams or spider's wishes.
She bit her lip, was silent,
And I hoped,
Nearly hoped she understood.
But then she named me James, Roger, and Magnicus,
While with her eyes cried, "Terror."

Then I laughed, because my kind do not weep,
Gave her skeins of gold, and fled the bitter day.

In the man—her captor, prince and husband—
I found no rival.
What could he know, palace born,
Of a girl who'd run in barefoot fields,
And scratched her shins on blackberry castles
For love of their sweet black gore?
And what could such a wild girl know

Of pantomime pageants and ballroom show
While footings rot beneath and the roof caves in above,
And how very much fine horses need to eat?
He would make of her chattel,
Whereas I would make her free as lightning fire
On a dry autumn hill.
Let her only once refuse to guess,
Let her but one morning keep her silence in trade for my gold,
And no iron bonds could keep her in.
But night on night the moon ate herself to blackness
And dawn upon dawn, my girl starved herself
Despite my offered feast.
Not Hector. Not Michael. Not Cobweb.

And so, in measured weeks I came to learn her truth
And could but mourn to know it true;
My girl of the fair, sweet tears and briar-tangled feet
Could never love me.
She was a creature made of fear, suckled to it
Fed upon it, wed unto it
Till love itself struck terror in her breast.
Oh yes, the love of the Sidhe is fearsome,
Wild, fierce, magnificent as a storm,
And fearful souls have learned to crave it before, but she,
My bruised cavern rose, my weeping willow,
Was bent and broken to the fear; trained to it, tamed to it
As a wild hawk hooded,
Eye-stitched into darkness till dreams of heaven fade,
And she thinks herself but a pretty toy
Upon a Prince's glove;
Freedom bespoke her in fear's voice,
Wrung name after name from strawberry lips unthinking.
Caesar, Gwyll, Nefarion,
Hobarth, Seamus, Absalom,
Every word for terror she had ever learned.

When the moon swelled thick again,
She was making names up, mashing syllables together
And hoping they'd stick,
Her tears steel sharp and rank with desperation.
And however oft I might repeat my vow,
She would always, always speak her night's guesses
With fear trembling sour behind her milk-sweet breath.
It was not that I did not want the girl,
For she was still as starving-fair as ice in summer's heat,
And I longed to see her fingers stained and sweet once more;
Only I realized, by the light of the late moon's widening grin,
That I was growing tired.

Only think, for a moment, Mayfly;
How weary to be always terrible!
'Tis diligent work—the flash of teeth, the predatory glare,
The thorny claws, a-swinging one's tail just so.
Exhausting.
I could not keep it up for even a pretty Mortal's span,
No matter her fate awaiting should our bargain fall her way.
Oh yes, even the Wildings of the Hill know what doom befalls
The rich-cream cow when she comes dry to milking.
I knew a day must come when her Spendthrift Prince
Would take hold of her udder only to find he must go thirsty.
And sorrowing, snickering, I could scent her fear-to-be,
Brought full to bitter fruit.
But her tear-spinning had grown stale as salt to me,
They streaked her cheeks like Bible ink, devoid of pearly shine
As she guessed me shriller and shriller.
Parksinon, Blix, Filibilocks.

"Woman, I will take you away,"
One final offer, straw bales tottering behind me
Beneath the hag's eye moon.
I did not give her time to speak, or to weep,
Or to beg for that which she had refused already,
But set about my mercy with a will.

Chambermaids are curious creatures, did you know?
This is why oft, we pinch them for it.
But peeking eyes and spying ears have their uses,
And a lilting inanity sung out of place—
A hollow tree, a chalk hole-hill, or the upstairs linens cupboard—
Why naught will draw a spying maid the quicker.
A simple song it was, such as a serving girl could learn
To sing without error in her Mistress' ear.
Out of a month's tedious golden whirl,
That grinding tune was worst;
To sing my name, the key to lock my girl's prison tight,
Couched in such pounding drivel, why
No hero of the Danaan strove the harder to endure!
I confess, I might have laughed
Just a little, from the stress.

That night, when I my teind delivered,
She met me in her prison;
My pearl girl, my petal,
Her blackberry fingers neat and folded in her lap,
Her bracken eyes smug with her doom.
"And have you guessed my name?" I asked her,
Wondering if her pride could bear

To lose our wager, and win the greater prize....
Well. That answer, of course, is well enough known;
Not Solomon. Not Zebedee.
Not free to run
In summer's gloaming all her days and dance
In bramble bowers beyond the reach
Of greedy Princes, foolish mothers, pointless, perilous tests, ah me
What fools these Mayflies be
To snatch the Ever After, leaving Happily behind.

And so we come unto it, friend;
The reason for my tale you surely guess
For I see the ghosts of brambles upon your booted feet
And stolen cherry summers on your lips,
And in this close prison room
Your moth-silk tears gleam like silver to me,
And happen I could love you.
A bit, perhaps, I do already.
So let us make our wager plain,
My apple-bright, my midsummer's morn;
I will take on your impossible task,
Be it spun, plowed, sorted, slain, sewn,
Retrieved from dragon's hoard or muddy well,
And I will give to you the seeming of success my dear, only
Only if in one moon's turn
You do not guess my name,
Then I swear it, human child,
I will take you away.

Grandfather

Dennis M. Lane

As a child he was supposed to have been my protector; 'Pops,' I called him.
To the world outside he was a smiling, kindly man; always the first to offer
a helping hand.

But I knew better....

Late at night, when Mother was at work, he would come to my room.
Tell me how much he loved me.
Explain how I could show that I loved him.

I was just a kid, what could I do?

After too many of these nights, I went to my mother, stood there
trembling....
Finally, I managed to spit it out, the filth that I'd endured, the horror

visited upon me in the dark.

And she refused to believe.
With dead eyes, eyes that could not meet mine, and with lying lips, she said that I must be mistaken. That Pops was a good man, and he loved us both.
Years later, I realized that Mother knew; that she too had endured visits in the dead of night.
But that could not excuse her.
She knew, and she could have stopped it, but fear, or shame, stopped her.

And so the visits continued.

When I was old enough, big enough to wield a knife, I dreamed of cutting off Pops' head; like that of an ogre in one of my storybooks.
But, deep down, I knew that the death of my grandfather would not take away the pain, would not end the nightmares.
I was broken; my soul could not be mended, and so I devised a plan.

Despised at school, ridiculed for always having my head in a book, I kept my head down.
I studied and I escaped the town that had been my prison.

Years passed by; years in which I rarely saw Mother, hardly ever saw Pops.
As colleagues went home for the holidays, there was no smiling family at the fireside for me.
I stayed in the lab, working, and the pieces came together.

Until, one day, the test rig disappeared!

Years of suppressing my tears, of not talking, came to my aid.
The test rig disappeared, and I didn't move, didn't shout in triumph.
I just smiled to myself, sure that my plan was near to fruition.

Pops was long dead, Mother was in a home, my fallen arches were a testament to a youth long flown.

But Pops still haunted my dreams, still caused me to wake up crying.
And he always would.

A long weekend, the laboratory empty as I assembled the components, parts of a machine that I had conceived decades before.
The other researchers had no idea what they had been working on, all those years.
No time for tests, no need for goodbyes; I set the dials, engaged the flywheel, and blinked out of existence.

<<<<<<<<<<<<<<<<<

The machine brought me here, to a familiar street.

I stand outside that house, a building that, to me, has always been full of darkness, and I'm surprised by how bright, how new, how *clean* it looks.

The comforting feel of the knife, smooth and cool against my flesh, reassures me as I walk up the path.
Theory talks about the Grandfather Paradox, but I don't believe it: what can the universe do?
Strike me down with lightning?
Propel me back to the lab?
I have travelled through time, and no theoretical restriction is going to stop me.

I walk up the path and past the apple tree, strangely small, newly planted by Pops, then I slip down by the side of the house and into the always open back door.

As I enter the kitchen Pops jumps to his feet.
I pull out the knife and he stops.

Unusually for him, he has no words, no slick excuses.
Words fail me too: not a day has gone by when I haven't thought about what I would say, how I would accuse my abuser; but now, here, there is nothing to say.

Before he has a chance to move, I strike.
The blade sinks deep and his face goes slack, the way Mother's face went slack, that day so long ago (*ago?*)
When I told her (*tell her?*)
What Pops had done.

The young-faced, smooth-faced, two-faced abuser slips silently to the floor; blood pooling around him.

As his heart flutters and slows, I feel my own heart fading, like the propellers of a plane struggling to bite on air too thin.
I wonder if, in that far-off old-people's home, Mother's heart is also fighting, straining to beat just one last time.

My blood-drenched hand seems to phase out of existence, flesh becoming transparent, while, on the floor, Pops gurgles once more.
And, as three hearts beat their last, I know that he will not touch my unborn mother, that he will never come to my bed, to break the child that I was.
And, in that last instant, before all is remade, I … smile.

Memphis Street Railway Co. v. Stratton: 1915

Elizabeth McClellan

Nelson took a night job as a watchman
assigned to keep an eye on the ditch
the company left in the middle of Poplar
down by Third Street
when the linemen went home.

There is only so long you can stare into a hole
in a darkening street before the mind wanders
to someplace abysmal, hears whispers of
Russians choking on German death,
the color and taste of the Divine Sarah's

gangrenous leg, every unattended woman
Typhoid Mary undercover, the apocalyptic portent
of six months of relentless locusts in the Holy Land
a buzzing swarm in his ears, something like
a knot of snakes down in the dark—

No job for a man,
to guard what no one wants,
when it can't run off,
get lost, get stolen—

hardly a fault to retreat to the shadow
of the church, contemplate warm things:
payday, suppertime, slow burn of corn whiskey,
a corner out of the wind to smoke in

until the world all goes to hell:
in a pit whispering filth in your ear
or until some bastard destroys your reverie:
a cannonfire bang, a lot of yelling.

Running around the corner Nelson saw
the young men in their shirtsleeves
gathered around his hole, half-full
of slightly crumpled Pierce-Arrow,

caught one of them in the act,
prying up the company's boards
while his friends smoked, laughed,
called out encouragement.

Nelson bellowed, "*Dammit,*
why the hell did you run your toy

into my ditch, you damn idiot?"

The man ignored him, kept going,
wrenched another plank loose,
contempt in his every move and glance.
No man should have to put up
with such affronts.
 It's all going to hell
in Pierce-Arrows and shirtsleeves and
soft work, tearing up my walk,
filling up my hole.

"You fucker, don't tear up my walk"

Nelson's pistol butt—a dull meteor—
exploded star-showers inside the intruder's skull,
sent man and board and blood flying
into the Arrow, screaming into the trench

laid out in First Presbyterian's shadow,
friends and onlookers gathered
 like mourners at graveside,
stink of exhaust mingled with
moonshine, copper, testosterone, dirt,
old mold, something sharp as ozone.

The cops socked Nelson in the mouth
before they threw him in the drunk tank
to moan all night for whiskey, keening
ey-ah ey-ah, yahsahgah
through swollen lips, bloody teeth.

The desk officer knew Meemaws,
had a Mamaw of his own, assumed
the drunk's swelled jaw was swallowing
his consonants. Some always will
call out for grandmother in their hurt.

Nelson showed up at First Pres every Sunday
after his sister bailed him out, got baptized,
quit drinking for real this time.

When the company fired him, even
before the lawsuit—he told his pastor,

"Brother, when I reach for the bottle now
I see the devil like a ball of snakes
wrapped up around it. I smell people's
livers dying. Now I know
what hell smells like."

He got up in church to thank the Lord
when the legislature impeached
the Memphis attorney general
on a tide of liquor flowing down Beale,
ignored the blue-flame looks
from those of his fellow holy elect
who voted dry and drank wet,

gloried in their measured contempt
for his excess zeal, repeated to himself

rejoice and be exceeding glad
for great is your reward in heaven, for so
they persecuted they the prophets
which were before you.

When Crump and Howse toppled,
he street-preached a while, then wended
his way out of Memphis, onto
the tent-revival circuit of the Delta,
his witness a small-town star attraction:

I said to the devil liquor eyah eyah
yahsahgah, an old Hebrew prayer
the Lord revealed to me,

something David strummed on
his old harp, something Paul and Silas
sang out in jail, all the long night

I tell you all
pray it with me now

and you'll see the devil when he comes
in the liquor and the women and
the corruption, the Lord

will show you your enemy
in the form of snakes
and you'll dance around

every trap that old devil
ever set for your blessed soul

let us pray

and when they came to him warm and sweet
flushed with tent-sweat, all over blessedness,
pure as virgins whatever they knew,
they were sent from God, not that rotten

scaly devil coiled around every clear mason jar,
every amber bottle from Lexington and Lynchburg
out to Nutbush and Bucksnort,
no snake-whispers in their holy mammal moans.

That was the summer the men got pregnant too,
eating six meals a day, weird bumps
in their middles, mockeries of their expecting
mamas and wives, so many babies
set to come along around February.

The math was avoided, by simple way
of common consent. Call it a miracle,
ignore the stomachs
stretched out of shape,
writhing forms beneath
the skin more like snakes

than the ripples of feet or elbows
passing across the bellies of the women
by Thanksgiving, whole families sitting
pushed back from the table swollen, shamed.

By the time someone thought to look
for that rascal of a preacher
who led them all to sin,

some tiny town living out hard times
on 'shine had hung him high,
left him for the birds, the tree-snakes,
the stinging flies. The babies came

all gray, pulled half-dead from their mothers
 but breathing too well not to save,
strange boneless toes be damned.
Their parents would sin no more,

and anyway, said the grandmothers,
they'll marry each other, see if they don't.

The husbands and the too-young men
waddled slow and bloated
until late March when the equinox
sent them staggering out to the fields,

vomiting knots of scaly snakelets
that slithered off, leaving no dust-trails,
only sour mouths, deflated dewlap stomachs,

a story mostly untold by the time

the smoke-colored infants learned
to toddle on those strange feet,

rearing up in an instant when
the babies began to speak, alien hisses
overlaying their syllables, raising
their brothers and sisters from
hidden holes in the earth.

Sci-Fi Memory

Glen Pape

The end of the world was so much more;
there were bonfires laughing along the shore.

A single red rose petal,
delicately curled along one edge,
billowed like the corner of a satin sheet
in the warm acidic wind.

Black flakes flickered down
like obsidian snow
falling from a coral sky.

The water moved imperceptibly closer.

With nature so stilled,
we could see each scale on the butterfly's wing—
how each was a canvas, each with a still life
painted in iridescent oil.

The end of the world was so much more:
the indignant rich and ceaseless poor

shared an exhausted peace
in the breathtaking silence
of barren fields.

The tents were pitched
in interlocking circles
and meandering lines,
the flaps pulled aside
to expose what lived inside—
chaos here, order there.

Small rosettes of young girls,
their arms on each other's shoulders,
stirred the dust with their bare feet and made it dance.

Their parents told elaborate stories,
sculpting the air with their hands as they spoke.

Once we heard a choir of sobs rise to a crescendo
until one broke away in a spellbinding aria.

Creation was everywhere.

The end of the world was so much more
than anything that came before.

How well do you remember?
Did the buildings really rise like fists
above low, dark clouds that never lifted?
Was there ever a mountain
where hawks spiraled through a gray sky for prey?
Did we honestly struggle for our love
on the raw vinyl stools of a cheap café,
or fight for our beliefs on crowded streets
cloaked in cigarettes and wine? I don't know.

I can only remember the darker scents that followed.

The end of the world was so much more
than padlocks hung from shattered doors.

At last, in the absence of signs,
there were no more rhymes for children.
Everything spoken was simple and pure.
Nothing meant more than it was.

When we looked each other in the eyes
we saw only the pulse, the burst of color,
the darting movements, the pupils opening.
There were no assumptions or hidden meanings.

When we touched, nothing stood between us.

The end of the world was so much more:
the slow breath of desire was everywhere,
the freedom of surrender.

The embrace of life was everywhere,
though not enough to hold back death.

Six Random Facts About Halley's Comet

Inspired by Suzanne Halley Dean's "Halley's Comet"

J. E. Stanley

1.

The Sun, like all stars, is male.
The comet, like all comets,
is female, a lover
orbiting her beloved,
burning in his presence,
then dying, again and again,
in the cold void of his absence.

Someday, she will burn away completely.
The Sun will take no notice.

2.

Once, Halley's Comet
passed too close to Pluto.
A minute piece broke off,
fell 3 billion miles to Earth.
On the spot where it landed,
a tree sprung from the soil,
a tree like no other, with leaves
that resembled blue flames
whenever the west winds would blow.

The tree was so beautiful
that it was cut down
and sold in pieces.

Centuries later, a small piece
ended up in the hands of Andrea Amati
who used it in his finest violin.
The instrument would play only melodies
of loneliness and exile
though no one knew why.

3.

Perihelion: 0.6 Astronomical Units,
closer to the Sun than the Earth will ever be.

Aphelion: 35.1 Astronomical Units,
farther than any human will ever travel,
though some may tell you otherwise.

For both Halley's Comet and humans,

distance
is always the most relevant variable.
That one thing, we have in common.

4.

Halley's comet becomes visible
approximately once every 28 blue moons.
"Approximately" because precision
is an abstract concept.
Nothing in nature is precise.
There is no truly straight line,
no perfect circle.

Besides, the blue moon isn't even blue
and has its own agenda.

5.

"Halley's Comet" is not its true name.
Its true name can only be written
in the language of the sky
and cannot be expressed in English
or, for that matter, any human tongue.

6.

The Sun, like all stars, is female.
The comet, like all comets,
is male, a lover
orbiting his beloved,
burning in her presence,
then dying, again and again,
in the cold void of her absence.

Someday, he will burn away completely
and the Sun will take no notice.

Objectifying Faerie

Jane Yolen

1. I Am the Apple

I am the apple
dappled by sun,
polished by rain
burnished by galls
cut by the witch,
stitched by her hand,

injected with poison,
suspected by none.

2. I Am the Spindle

I am the spindle,
winding the yarn,
prepping the spinning
that brings you much harm.
I am the prickle
disturbing your sleep,
leaving your mother
and father to weep.

3. I Am the Red Cloak

I am the red cloak,
redder than a cardinal on a branch,
more rouged than a whore's lips,
pinker than a virgin's cheeks,
more crimson than a rose in snow,
more brilliant than the sunrise, sunset,
more final than heart's blood
spilled across a sheet.

4. I Am the Bridge

I am the bridge,
over the spume,
over the river's rush,
over the womb,
over the cataract,
over the fall,
over the grave.
There is always a toll.

5. I Am the Pea

I am the pea,
under the bed,
the itch, the wish,
the sound in your head,
the uneasy question,
the dream that you dread,
the royal pain carried
until you are dead.

6. I Am the Glass Slipper

I am not squirrel fur, from under the chin,
nor kid's leather made from belly skin,

nor alligator slashed from the tail,
nor snake skin hung upon a rail,
nor pony's hide stretched taut and fine,
nor mink's fur: soft priceless shine.
I am the glass unforgiving,
meant to cut your feet to ribbons.

7. I Am the Book

I am the book,
open I lie;
closed, revealed
to the naked I.
Truth in telling,
truth behold.
I am the book
if truth be told.

The Last Wife

Jennifer Crow

Easy to say, "Leave the key in the drawer."
Easy, when your own house has no locked doors,
When stairways don't rise to forbidden corridors,
When your handsome and thoughtful spouse
Doesn't shut that rosewood box
When you walk in the room.
Easy to give advice you'd never have to take,
Like bitter medicine on another patient's tongue.

I tasted mysteries at an early age, drank secrets
With my mother's milk and heard her cry
On afternoons when I came in early from the park.
So when he knelt, blue-black beard
Waxed to a fine point, dark eyes beseeching,
I took his hand and his secrets as my own.

No one tells you, at the altar or before, that 'worse'
Always comes after better, that secrets
Stink like the dead until you can almost hear the stench
Walking room to room, in that hallway
You never enter. I was weak—not then, but before,
When I sat in the parlor with a book open on my knee
And tried not to look at that rosewood box—I admit
My weakness, for I wanted so to believe the dream.

Truth is its own kind of strength, the biting draught

You take when the lies lose their flavor. I pressed the cup
Of it to my lips, swallowed it to the dregs, licked my lips
So no drop could escape me. I drank to the memory
Of a closed box, a closed heart, and then I took
That key
That brass key with its patina of old stains
That heavy, cold key
And I committed the inevitable sin.
Faithless, I climbed the stair.
Heartless, I opened the lock.
Hopeless, I touched each bony brow in turn,
Named them from the diaries on the shelf.

You know the rest. Otherwise, you wouldn't be here
With your dogs and shovels, your mistrustful stare.
Yes, I waited for him at the top of the house,
With my dead sisters behind me for courage.
I waited there, and when his heavy tread shook
The house, I raised that iron bar over my head,
And I brought it down. I brought him down
In the wreckage of his secrets, and my sisters—
My dead sisters, ranged in rows behind a brass lock—
Wept ashy tears. What, then, will you do to me?
What can you do to me, when I have seen the worst
Men can do to women, when I am witness
To the cruel passions they call love?
You may have a key, sir,
Cold metal to turn in an iron-banded door,
But I have my sisters for company,
And my heart in a rosewood box.

Their Cold Eyes Pierced my Skin
Jenny Blackford

Two years ago, my reputation was as clean as yours.
It wasn't *safe*—
a woman's name's not safe until she's dead,
sometimes not even then—
but it was safe enough. The young men of the village
and their tender peach-like buttocks
never moved me, nor did the girls,
however soft their hair or bright their eyes,
nor the worn-out husks of older folk,
tired from scrabbling out their lives
on our unforgiving stony mountainside
far from Mycenae.

But the two centaurs who hunted in the valley,
the year I turned eighteen—
oh, they were different,
alive and free.

Their hair curled down their backs like wild black waterfalls;
their cold eyes pierced my skin.
My fingers ached to comb their tails,
to smooth their strongly-muscled flanks.

I told no one, of course. Who could I tell?
My virtuous ever-weaving aunt? No.
I could not even whisper at my mother's grave,
sorrowing her ghost.

Two years ago, as I have said, my name was clean. These days,
the gossips in the street need only point
at the spring grass under the trees,
and the boy child who frolics there: my son.
But they don't know the half of it.

I succumbed, not to a local man or youth,
but to the lure of shining hooves
and glossy hides. Of course, there's more:
for any mountain girl who's ever milked a ewe or two, perhaps a goat,
has seen the ram or he-goat led to her in spring,
his huge balls heavy in their leather sack.
My centaurs were the same: formidable.
I loved them both, inseparably, as they loved me
And one another.

So, for a time, I truly lived.
My centaurs hunted hare and deer; I tickled fish;
I learned their summer songs, and danced with them, and drank their wine,
lolling on soft sweet grass far from my father and his farm—
but autumn came.
I saw the two I loved watching the birds make arrows in the sky
as they flew south;
soon my horse-men must go,
wild things that they were.
They stroked my hair and kissed the rounding mound
low on my abdomen: our child.
I cried and sulked, and was a fool.
They sang me songs of long-ruined palaces,
of stars fallen to earth,
of queens who wept gold tears.
I would not go with them;
they could not stay.

My lovers galloped south. I lingered for a month,
sure they would return for me—their love—
but I was wrong.

When winter came, I had no choice.
I walked the bitter path, stony and steep, back to my father's house.
Despite his threats, I would not name the man who took my honor.
How could I have?

The priestess shook her head, when in my fear
I asked what to expect: a foal,
to turn my father's world completely upside down? A boy?
The goddess could not be second-guessed, she said;
children bring joy and pain.
I had not hoped for much;
her own mind has been hazed with sorrow,
since the night her daughter went to the naiads' spring,
and did not return.

After my longest day and night of pain, my aunt held up my baby boy:
ten tiny fingers, ten tiny toes.
No curling mane, no swishing tail.
Life would be easier for him that way, I knew.
But when I closed my eyes
and touched his feet,
I felt not baby flesh but tiny hooves.
I smiled a secret smile.
My boy. *Our* boy.

I weave and spin, as women must, and look out from the door
as my son scampers on the grass
under the oaks.
Is that a tail flicking in the sun?
I blink and it's not there.
I blink again, and smile to see
his shining hooves.

String Theory

John Philip Johnson

My friend is telling me a story.
As he talks, I'm thinking about string theory.
I have gone over to his desk.
He wants to loan me a movie, an old VHS.
He is telling me a different story.
He is telling me now the story behind the story.
We're with a correspondent in World War II.

We're in the Vatican archives.
The court of Tiberius, who has just died.
As he talks I'm thinking about the story
of a life being pulled across the moment now.
There is one word, one sound,
of, he says, or said, or is saying,
I'm looking at his fleshy lips say *of*,
nothing else is moving,
but he has already said *of course*,
already gone on and is saying something else;
and I suddenly see this instant we live in
as the curl of time scraping across his lips,
the fourth dimension bent over us like an edge
moving through the house of three dimensions.
If I try to hold on to one word, one moment,
it splinters into shards
and what is real makes no sense.

I could have said the meat of three dimensions,
I did before. Here, or later, I'm thinking
about aboriginals drawing curlicues in sand.
I'm thinking about the white clouds
of what could have been, farther away, much softer
and more intricate than the thing touching his lips.
I am thinking of Francis of Assisi, bi-locating because
he believed so much. I'm thinking our understanding
is drawn down to a single point of indeterminate size,
condensed and then uttered as a short word,
and then we are washed over the falls.

No one, my friend is saying, about a document
that may or may not have existed,
no one really knows for sure, but,
he says, and *of course* he says again
and he has gone on and is saying something else now
and I'm thinking how things are stretched out
as far as the east is from the west,
how what he has said or might have said
or said in some other way or couldn't say
is clustered around him, intersecting discretely on his lips,
six or seven dimensions kissing him—

I'm thinking how all the dimensions and worlds
are clustered here, from their myriad beginnings
banging to their various apocalypses, present,
including the ones that are nothing but bulk
or the ones that are dream chambers or the ones
that are like the spider plant on his desk,

how they become a single thought of indeterminate size
which we don't have a word for but is the husk
for all these things; I'm thinking how my friend and I
are like musical strings, vibrating in this fascinating place,
how we are like everything else, how it is all
like a single word, poised half-said, a word resting,
a word identical to its self-pronouncing lips,

and,
and I'm thinking of the worlds and the possible worlds,
more worlds still, including the ill-conceived ones,
including the ones that are nothing but bulk,
including the ones that are dream chambers,
that render all the other worlds into dreaming,
dreams drawn to the utmost point of indeterminate size,
and I'm thinking the thought of myriad beginnings
banging into various apocalypses and changes of heart,
like the words inflating from my friend's mouth,
being said and then disappearing; and I'm thinking
of the myriad worlds that stretch from other worlds,
the possible worlds and the ill-conceived ones, including the ones
that are only the slightest of rims around nothing,
and I'm thinking of how my friend and I are like musical strings,
vibrating in this fascinating and seemingly endless symphony,
I'm thinking how we are like everything else, how it is all drawn
to a single point, a word, resting, half-said, like the word *of*,
poised on self-pronouncing lips, poised in the half-listening
dream chambers, the ones that render all the other worlds
into dreams, dreaming drawn down to the utmost point,
rendered like music, like the vibrations of a single word.

A Midsummer Night's Dream

K. C. O'Malley

How shall I love you?
Can I find a way? In our
constant journeyings
have our paths crossed once too often?
Do we meet again
to see if it is safe to say
goodbye?

How I have missed you—
your hands, your lips
your eyes in the morning
your song coming up through

                              the darkness
Fireflies gleam and fade
and baby rabbits munch in clover
wild birds eat out of your hand
and rain water runs
                    off your back
                    and down along your thighs

For many years I have
kept a place for you
in my heart's shadow
          No one can see it
          neither you nor I

And for many years I have carried a longing
—and even now I dream
of just once telling you the story
sitting you down one cold winter's evening
with a cozy chair, a fire, a jug of hot cider

But when I dream with you
                    the heroine always dies
                    or comes to a bad end
                    the snow doesn't stop for three days
                    men in black coats and fat cigars come
                    out of the woods and surround the house
                    and no one escapes
The audience leaves in tears

I dream
of banners aloft: clashing
trumpets announce my entrance
all juicy and sizzling
decked with parsley and an
                              apple in my mouth

But with you
          I am always a little underdone
          and have bitten a piece of the apple

If nothing in the world can match our love
how shall we live
now that we are gone from it?

Two little girls in the farmyard:
you killed the chickens for the family's dinner
your sister was afraid
Later you crossed the desert alone
and brought back a Hollywood husband

that sort of thing was not done
Now you walk in protected forests
uprooting poison ivy, teaching
virtue to the third generation. While I ...

I stalk the cities and highways
in search of your head

with long experience
my blade is sharpened to a fine edge

my tracks lead to your door

I will be waiting by the back stairs
underneath the ailanthus
I am coming
tonight

Sweet Mercy, Her Body an Ark of Wild Beasts

Kelly Rose Pflug-Back

> *There are dead who light up the night*
> *of butterflies,*
> *and the dead who come at dawn*
> *to drink your tea*
> *as peaceful as on the day your*
> *guns mowed them down.*
>
> —*Mahmoud Darwish*

My life has been the tin ribbons of a jaw harp,
its bent notes twanging
in the lightless space cupped between my hands.
I've tried to make sense of it:
the button eyes of cloth animals,
frayed cotton straining
at their herniated stitches.
The bones of my face are a map, I told you
the plates of my skull fused like petals at my crown
where the Queen's infantry anointed me in mortar dust
and closed their ranks forever.
I told you the truth:
before I knew you, I lived for years as a sin eater.
Beauty was a charm I would never inherit,
my palate's cracked seam a cleft between floorboards
in the attic apartment
where we lived before the war.
You never stared at the palimpsest of scrawled transgressions
that I was sure still etched my body.
Once you took my hand

and pressed it to the shallow depression in your skull
where you told me famine had wracked you while the bones were still soft.
Trepanned from birth,
your fontanelles like spy-holed fingers
never quite closing
over the keyhole to a locked room.
As a child, you told me how you used to wake sometimes
to see a wax museum of saints looming above your bones' cradle
the dark-haired Virgin standing over you,
her robes a swimming quilt of fish and birds.
Their feathers were cursive, crested
in halved suns;
she pressed her palm to your chest, once
and fear died inside you.
I wonder where the mark of her hand is now
watching hoarfrost bloom against the panes
of a shattered city.
The world turns its black spokes,
and the wind covers my tracks forever.
Daylilies wilt and bow their heads,
blight-palsied stalks
curling, clawed against my palm.
The insult of bayonets will erase you
a limp body left to bear witness
to history's bloody unfolding.
I am a corpse, like the others
they heap like sandbags
along the edges of their barricade.
I am a man who has blinded himself
painting portraits on eggshell fragments
with a single-hair brush,
touching the clothes you left folded in my room
until their texture no longer recalls your body
and my hands, too are cast into the insensate dark.
In my mind
I called you Lost.
I called you City of Ur.
Your eyebrows the dark arches of Fayoum portraits,
the bones of whales' ancestors scattered through the floors
of now-parched Cretaceous seas.
The stelae of their backbones rise like buzzard-ridden arbors,
spines whip-stitched, lacing between sun-bleached dunes.
I want the ululations of a thousand throats
to guide me across black waters whose shores I'll never reach
a ghost of night overpasses
watching the headlights of transport trucks pass through my body
before the dark under the train bridge swallows them again.

I want to open my eyes to see her staring down on me
from the grotto tattooed on your sunken chest
frail and impossible, a hothouse flower
blooming in the nuclear heat.
I have bled, and seen a river fork through this place.
I have watched lithograph smoke
spill from the barrels of silenced guns
to curl in bows and lariats
around her heart-shaped face;
fetal buds pushing through cracked asphalt,
the bones of plowshares rusting
in soil too anemic for even the grass to anchor its roots in.
Somewhere, a revolution is happening
that will never be broadcast.
Somewhere, the sun rises on a world
no longer drawn as if by some hand
enamored
of human pain.

Lucubration

A composition that smells of the lamp …

Kyla Lee Ward

A most perplexing paradox, to write
so late at night with such a light as this
banishing darkness from the magic ring;
but day thoughts are not night thoughts, so this hiss
of warming gas and stink of burning dust
must be the very consecrated 'cense,
the silver inlay and the mighty name
that lets me press the demon with a slim,
unsure advantage. Is this but his play,
awaiting chance to reft my soul away?
Still I would summon darkness! That each door
and window, underside and crack extend
into the furthest reaches of the 'byss,
all that has been, may come to be and is.

It seems that I have stalked tenebral paths,
leaves pressing thick and bends obscuring sight.
Only the scent of cereus and of rose
to mark the way: the velvet brush of moss
and kiss of web assurance of retreat.
This is my victim's garden, well beyond
the outer wall yet feel I still no fear—
a mask and blade ensure my welcome here.

To move so swift, so silently and sure!
No thorn ensnares, no twig betrays my step;
the grace of darkness speeds me to our tryst
in empty passage, else his very bed.
No matter whose the coin that bought this death,
of all that call this rotting city home,
there shall be heat, a muffled scream and blood
sweet on my lips, for I am nothing more
than wolf or 'pard, or any other bane
they seek to keep beyond the palisade.
Close now, all unaware my prey awaits,
a turn, and through the shivering of fronds
and shattering of water, there is light.

I see them through the arches where they dance
gilded by harpsichord and violin,
silvered by laughter and flirtatious glance;
none look without. To them the world is all
a crystal ball that catches candlelight
and sends motes spinning, hand in tender hand.
In peacock satin, broidered and bejewelled,
their faces masked as panther, wolf or skull
and he, 'tis surely he who thus affects
assassin's black, a blatant mockery.
For I must never stray within the light,
the legendry of my cruel craft maintain,
no partner take, save in the dance of death;
this code enshrined, yet how may I refrain?
Why do I stalk these sightless alley-ways
but for a glimpse of life's rose aureole?
Why take their coin and venture in their sphere
if not to touch all that I was denied
when fate cast me upon the darker shore?
I dance upon a dagger every night!
Why should I not dance here amongst the crush
of hip and shoulder, lacing lip and thigh?
How could they tell my visage from their own?
So entered I, and soon the answer learned,
such answer as permits the gods to laugh,
such grace I had as lay beyond the dance;
where others faltered, I descried the tune,
nor caught a foot, nor brushed a careless hand
in weaving ever closer to my prey:
oh laughing gods, unravel how it may
be grace itself that gave myself away?
Questions assail me, laughter closes ranks
and hems me in. I can see nothing past
the light but light permits them to discern

the deed undone and mark, it is for that
I die, beyond a hundred crimson crimes.
Now as my judges bring the rod and flame
I cry for darkness, prodigal in shame
and only dread the work that they now do
will leave life's final shackle on my wrist.
All I have been brought screaming down to this.

Thus I retreat, and seek throughout the vast
for certain sanctum and yet deeper dark.
It seems I have walked colonnades aside
of hornéd heads with women's breasts, and known
a man's face rise above a lion's paunch,
serpents and scarabae with human hands
and phalluses: I say, not all were stone.
Across the sands disguising all above,
devoutly, pilgrims trace an ancient path
from out the lesser shadows of the night,
down cunning stairs that lead to us below.
Echoing vaults as chill and black as death,
where barques of granite draw their cargo nigh,
and stone papyrus hold the heavens high.
Our oracle brings men with azure beards
and layered robes, redheads with pallid skin,
bronze men and black: with offerings of wood,
of iron and silver, ivory and salt,
the oil of whales and one thing more, for here
no circle holds the demon kind at bay.
The supplicants pass columns in the murk,
offering bodies to a winged embrace
and throats to kisses bringing such sweet pains
as only teeth permit and blood contains.
They come for knowledge: knowledge they shall find
in scented smoke that frees the untrained mind,
murmured by shades and hissed by coiling fiends,
and whispered from the lips of blessed things
that pass above them, stirring fragrant wind.
Whate'er they seek, be it the fate of kings,
the course of wars, felicity of brides,
or cure of plagues: the answer here abides.
Yet none of these shall ever find the lake
where lotus blossoms raise their scented heads
above black waters, warm and thick as blood.
None shall approach the greatest mystery,
the beating stone, the nigresence within
the inmost shrine, where only priests may go.
Only the chosen: all these paths are mine.

Yet still there is a thing that troubles me:
dogging my step and stinging in my eye.
Not ghost nor genius, yet it flits along
the colonnade, a disc both flat and fleet.
I fail to catch it: then as I pursue
I recognise intrusion from above.
Within the ceiling gleams a single hole
and through that hole there lies a shining world
of tincts known only through their dying fall,
of sounds and scents, of trees and fields of grain,
loud rivers flowing underneath a sky
where rides a god that shows himself to all.
I am of those who see without their eyes,
kept from the world to force the subtle sense:
and though I now imagine sight and sound
and quake within, I know my duty well.
With sleeve across my face, a fragile mask,
I seek out proper servants for the task
of sealing up this breach of sanctity.
Had I but looked, perhaps I would have seen
the doom that was foretold us long ago
approaching now. Perhaps I could have been
the saviour of some shard, and wrought a fate
somehow less cruel, and kept our memory
intact for all the ages yet to come.
The dust sifts down, and yet I see it not.
The columns creak, yet I walk on until,
with booming shriek and rushing tide of sand,
the stony heavens split apart in flame
and men descend who seek no wisdom here.
The spirits shriek and yet they hear them not.
The monsters writhe but they can only see
statues adorned with gold and many gems
run molten in the furnace of the day.
All I might be is given to decay.

Once more, once more I flee into the dark
and, shrieking, seek out such a potent form
as may defend the fragments of my soul.
No weakness now, of either love or fear.
This blade I bear is forged of ancient shards.
This mask I wear was stolen from a tomb.
Armour I carry, and an evil name,
that Christian priests may use to conjure hate.
I am the wolf's right hand, the raven's throat,
who rises from the forests of the north
where endless run the trees whose blackened trunks
and gloomy branches scarify the sun

and men mistake the days for nights until
dread madness seize them, else they chance on me.
I come now, from the necromantic groves
as crest of storm devouring the bright day
and all the slaves in fields and cities quake:
their devil curse, that loosed me on the world.
Their devil, ha! They'd better blame their God.
Dreadful the sacrifice that has allowed
my conjuring, and it was not my hand
which spilled the blood across the altar stone.
In my ranks heretics and rebels crawl
who lost their lives upon the block or wheel,
and lovers slain for loving past the bounds,
proud pagans Roma never held in thrall,
the charcoal husks of witches, and yet more:
monsters and prodigies of form possessed
to make of man's perfection but a jest.
All share my hunger to extinguish light
and in this final victory to rest.

"O hear me now, you captives of the hour!
Yes, hear me now, you blind and shackled fools!
Prepare to welcome all you have despised.
The cross shall not avail you, nor the scourge.
Embrace us, love the grand catastrophe,
for by this turn or death, you shall be free!"
Walls crumble hissing into ancient sand
at my bare touch; the sputtering cannon dies
at merest glance, and where I tread the grass
is blackened and the earth gapes wide and births
yet more abominations at my call.
So die the knights, their armour but a glove
to animated tendrils of the dark;
so die the priests, their chastity consumed
by laughing nightmares, bringing bliss with fangs;
so die the mothers, shrieking out their right
to mercy to rough things of stone and clay
that never knew the pressure of the womb.
So die they all, and every child who cries.
The beacon fires, lanterns of the watch,
the flambeaux that illumine all the State,
the great cathedral seeming to contain
within a rose of glass the very sun,
now one by one, they die. All die and night
comes sweeping through the city like the tide,
the final flood that never shall recede.
One light remains within the highest tower,
one light alone, and this both faint and far,

but I'll not leave my vengeance incomplete.
My best companions running at my heels
and screeching in my wake, I take the stair
that circles ever upwards, ever on.
The light's a grin that mocks my every step!
The light's an eye that sees my deepest pain.
The light: the light is no more than a lamp
that casts a circle round a desk and chair,
and adumbrates the figure seated there
with pen in hand. And yet somehow in this
I see creation's round and all that is.

If I wrote in the darkness, the result
would be such scratchings and strange hieroglyphs
that any passing eye would think no more
than random marks, the proper work of flies
or imbeciles. If such the demon is,
my own self come to steel me to this task,
the greater soul of which I am the part
that weeps, my duty nonetheless is clear:
complete the work that is my purpose here,
as I return to darkness, so to light,
without whose hissing breath, I cannot write.

Tell Them

after Carvens Lissaint

Lauren Banka

When I am dead,
when the snakes and the beetles come to take my body away,
after you have spent a year in silence sewing shirts out of driftwood
and the pilgrims come to you with bloody feet to ask of me,

her glory, they say
her aura, they say
the glittering light that shone from her ears,
the dark flame of her hair,   they say, tell them

I was all this and less. Tell them
my bones were made of packing foam
which stank to Hell in the summer and melted in the wet winters.
Tell them the shovel of my jaw was full of brass bearings,
sweating and fighting in the mosh pit of my mouth,
my throat a BB gun, that I used to spit them sizzling
at the faces of my closest friends. Tell them I was a fast learner.
Tell them my aim improved each time you saw me.

Tell them my eyes were shotglasses I asked everyone to refill.
Tell them I broke all my mirrors, just so I could have more mirrors.
Tell them you could always find me near mirrors, staring into gloss,
recognizing myself nowhere. Tell them I made too many promises
and too few secrets to ever keep any of either. When they ask you of me,

her tongue, they say,
it was a yellow hydra, wasn't it,
and its five heads spit bitter, spit salty, spit sweet and spicy and strong,
and each head with twelve teeth,
and each tooth with a single cavity,
and in each cavity a tiny pearl,
and in each pearl a tiny door,
and in each pearl a truth,   wasn't it?
wasn't it just like that?
                                        You tell them

a truth that can fit in a door in a pearl in a cavity in the mouth
of one fifth of anyone's hydra tongue is a useless truth. Tell them
I spit pearls at people too, and nobody thanked me for it,
and nobody should. Tell them I made them in my gut, swallowed
every irritant anyone sprayed, swallowed my own phlegm,
and clutched myself,
and hardened.

And when they stop asking questions. When their hearts
are vomiting a little in their own heart mouths, and they have just realized
how lost they are,
in a foreign country,
with bloody feet, they will ask you this:

but what about her size? We have heard
that she fit inside a mustard seed,
that her hammock was a half a walnut shell,
that she wore infant's shoes her whole life long,
that she flew for free in a carry-on bag,
that she didn't grow after age eight,
that she didn't grow after age fourteen,
that shirts were dresses on her and capris, full-length pants,
that she had to look up to talk to children,
that she had to look down to talk to her uncles,
that she beanstalked over tall men,
that she could barely fit into most buildings,
that you had to hold meetings outside if you wanted her to come,
that she held her closest friends in her pocket
that she held power tools and sawdust in her pocket
that she held the continents stacked like baseball cards
        in her pocket.

Tell them. Tell them I was all this and I was all this
and I was all of this. Tell them a third time
of my bitter anger, my hydra fury, my spitting mad.
Tell them I was small enough to fit in a brass bearing.
Tell them I scarred anyone who ever spoke to me,
that they carried my weight in their cheek. Did tricks
with it, when they wanted to flirt. Tell them how everyone left,
that they were right to. How these anchors of my anger
drifted like galaxies expanding, and the shortest distance
between one brass bearing and another was me,
and the longest distance between pearl and pearl was me.
Tell them how small I was. Tell them how large I was. Tell them
how small I still was. Tell them I took shots, and the world
was not always better for it. Tell them I left scars. Tell them
you can still see the mark.

The Horror at Fox Hollow

Lesley Wheeler

Fur prickled, pulse in a stutter, Kit turns off
the highway onto country roads. The woods
gleam between the fields—each gap a soft
unsettled mood shaped by walls that have stood,
       stone-faced, for hoary decades. From time to time
       she slows to squint at her notes by dash-light. Good
that she's alone. Her husband and son would team
       up to tease her for resisting GPS.
       But she won't get lost: Kit has print. Her beams
pick out the signs—and a sly possum, and a mess
       of dead doe gnawed by a dim thing that scurries away—
       so she follows her lines to Fox Hollow School for Girls.
An avenue of trees. Each raises a splay
       of dead fingers where blossoms should be. A guard
       in a bright-lit hut, clean-shirted, a scribble of gray
combed over his scalp, limps out. "Katherine Rennard,"
       she tells him, "here for the Poetry Festival."
       He steps back, rings someone, then waves her forward.
Belated panic thrills her. She could roll
       up her window, hang a quick K-turn, and go.
       A reading for two hundred teens? Too brutal.
But now she's trapped. There, under the glow
of security lights, waits the spunky teacher,
scarlet with enthusiasm for his not-too-
famous poet: tomorrow's special feature.
       Tonight, just listening. She's come mid-event,
       the Student Slam, and ducks into the bleachers.

No one heeds her; their whispery heads are bent
      together, in rows, at tables, in the furtive
      poses plotters take when poised to torment
their sisters. *It's a secret. Don't want to hurt*
      your feelings but. My god what is she wearing.
      Not aimed at Kit but it's easy to revert—
sneer down at her own wrinkled self, her timid bearing.
      Still the odd one. Masked. The teacher's pet.
      It's not a true slam—no one scruffy or swearing,
but all are keen, straining the leash. That edge.
      Two half-grown, trembling girls, their meter poor,
      recite a piece together, giggling, and get
off the stage before they hear the abysmal score.
      Someone still in riding breeches shakes
      her auburn tresses and declaims a more
successful paean to her horse. She likes
      to wring the cheers from slender throats. The winner,
      toothy, bites off an ode to midnight snacks.
The scene is gothic. Kit knows this tale of horror:
      a stranger comes to town. Folks seem normal—
too normal. She suppresses an improper snicker.
As it ends, a meager fog descends, miasmal.
      Kit's brought to a vacant guesthouse for the night.
      It's an ancient pile. The rooms are queer and dismal.
She nudges the doorstop aside—a crouched thing, not
      quite canine, made of metal—unzips her bag,
      hangs up her reading outfit, finds a note
from her son, tries to phone. Reception's bad,
      so the nature-poet draws her blinds against
      the mumbling trees, the silent huddled birds.
There's an oval portrait on her wall amidst
      the paper's tangled ivy: the mug of a fox,
      wary, studying the long-dead artist.
Kit finally dozes after testing the locks.
      Do the dreams bring on the fear or does the fear
      bring on the dreams? *A forest clearing. The clock's*
insect tick. She and her poetry books premiere
      on a low stage, fixed in the spotlight. She knows
      the risers are stocked with voyeurs. They leer at her
til dawn, when she rinses off the helplessness
      and hears her host's horn sound. The handles on
      his car are useless from the inside. "That noise,"
Kit asks. "Is it dogs?" "The baying of the hounds,"
      he gamely replies. "During these winter weeks
      the girls just love a fox-hunt." He parks, walks round
to let her out. "Don't worry, they're sated," he jokes.
      The earth is pocked and fragrant, deeply scored

by hoof and pad and other illegible tracks.
The master leads her on a walking tour
        of campus—a moss-veiled dorm, the spiffy gym
        for that twenty-first-century tone—and recounts some lore
of miscellaneous hauntings. Best, in the grim
        cafeteria, he gestures to a portrait of
the founder, vigorous and slim,
a coil of ghostly smoke floating above
        her hand, though the brandy and lit cigarette
        are painted out. Finally, at a remove
from the other buildings, the venue. And wild regret,
        as always, that she's agreed to this. Either way,
        whether the reading's triumphant or painful, Kit
will feel chagrin. There's something about a stage
        that alienates a person from herself.
As if, she thinks as she dog-ears some pages,
half-attending to the introductory riff,
        I'm not just the fox but the pack of hounds, too.
        And it's time for the beasts to be cast into the rough.
She wonders what she'll see from the lectern—a few
        well-mounted, vicarious hunters, checking her over?
Or slavering fangs? By instinct, she leaps at her cue.

—Here the fragment ends; the contriver
        of the ominous verses left them unfinished, unsigned.
        I return the scrap of foolscap to its clever
covert: a frayed edition left behind
by some other traveler. In the middle
of a journey, lost in a wood, the Fox Hollow kind.
Lovecraft would find "a hideous cult of nocturnal
        worshipers ... a revolting fertility-rite."
        Intense seclusion can make a visitor smell
like lunch. But then, I can be Kittish. A night
with no hounds is bad enough. A prep-
school is always grounds for dread: those bright
young flames when I'm halfway to ash; their up-
        wardly mobile predation; the descent
        into girl-world. Where my courage slips
and I surrender, though, is in the event.
        That servile play at status. My will and its teeth.
        And no one real—just ambience and scent.
Look up at the window and there she is, past death,
        translated, a monstrous shimmer in the pane
        where my reflection should be. Flushed out. Both
our mouths ajar. And then, her revenant grin:
        no gap now between think and say, want and eat.
        Devoured, she's whole. And listening for her kin.

we come together we fall apart
Lisa M. Bradley

I. Abe

Three sisters, then.
It was easier that way.
You wouldn't think
so many mouths
could hold one secret.
But it was a big secret
and deadly.
Six sets of lips and teeth
barely kept the thrashing thing in check.
And what our mouths couldn't hold
we gripped tight in nails and fists.

We were a young man
let loose in the world
'cause Daddy wrapped his hands
'round Mama's neck
one last time
made fists we couldn't scrape away
so she closed her eyes
in red-rimmed relief
never woke again.
We ran, but for years
we dreamed we were still there
lip split and nails bloody
cowering in the corner of forever.

We would've been better
released into the wild
than that mining town.
But it was as far as our legs could run
—we only had two back then.
No wolves in woods or nightmare
were half so ravenous as
the miners' wives. They coal-eyed
our smooth skin, our clean and nimble fingers.
They stroked our back unbent
chewed our kisses
licked us hard and soft again.
They swallowed our seed like
sweet stinging whiskey
hotter than their husbands' ash.

Honest work was no use.

What fences could be mended
what wells dug
when those women uncurled
the hammer from our fist,
the shovel from our palm?
But they kept us clean and fed.
We would've kept their secrets forever
—no soot on the sheets—
had it not been for our own.

Remember: so big and wild and deadly
and still so new.
It needed to be held
between teeth; it needed
to be pinned to the ground
its ruff clenched in a master's grip...
kind of like we wanted him
to take us:
That man in the bar
with the cards in his hands
all hearts and spades
and the whiskey-shine in his eyes
his pick-axe jammed into our chest
cracking our ribs apart
to finger at our heart.

II. Marguerite

Three brothers, then.
At least
that's what they said.
And who would've doubted them
as alike as they were?
Like chokecherries boiled thrice
the red dye growing fainter every time.

We didn't align by age.
Adelita was in trouble
and she needed an older man
unhindered by whispers
to save her name.
Not to mention
even then, belly rounding
she wouldn't wed a man
who wouldn't bed her hard and regular.
So she took Abe
and I, the eldest
married the next, Micah.
Camille, our little sister

sang a song of gathering
before her vows with Connor
to bind us.

I never had children
but no matter
I'd always had my hands full
with Adelita
and now I had her babe.
(How the happy couple slept,
I'll never know;
many a night I trekked
the path between our houses
unable to ignore
poor Dolly's wailing
a minute more.)

And if Micah never quite looked at me
as Abe did Adelita
well, our farm had six new hands
eager for honest work, even
Micah's, despite his smooth, soft skin
his clean and nimble fingers.
And I had my pride:
Micah's back unbent
his neck supple as whiskey?
They were safe from whip and noose
because he married me
Saint Marguerite.

III. Micah

We still remember that man at the bar.
He knew how to hold a pick-axe
but he was the mine owner's son
so he never had need.
Those canny hands of his
cupped his cards, all spades and hearts
caressed the air and we watched
till the back of our neck burned
for his phantom yoke
our lap warmed for his leash.
He laughed
and the whiskey-loosed bitterness
tugged through our pants, made us
thicker and hotter than the gropings
of any greedy miner's wife.

A bar girl saved us

when words turned rough
when threats unraveled the thickness
overtaking the card table.
The other players tried to club us
and the owner's son, for we were
of a kind: eye to eye, hand to hand
axe to aching heart.
Shielded by his daddy's money
he dodged sledgehammer fists
and insinuation, did nothing
but fold his hand and tilt his chair
to watch the girl pull us upstairs
for our "appointment."

But once we reached her bedroom,
she shoved us at the window.
"Get gone if you love life,"
she said, "and don't come back.
No miner's son wants to see
his eyes in you
and no mine owner's son
will cry if you die
making rope-ripe eyes at him."

So again we ran as far as our legs
could carry us
—just two legs back then—
and we risked wolves and winter's wind
to sleep in the woods.
But rest outran our double-soul
and our darkness bulged with nightmares
long as the leash we trailed
and certain as a noose.

IV. Adelita

Some might've mistaken Micah
for the handsome one.
Marguerite sure did.
Never did a woman take such pride
in matters she had so little to do with.
The way she coddled my daughter
—forever carried her between our houses
though the men paved the path
door to door; before,
because Dolly's shoes would get muddy;
then, because she might slip on the stones.

Just so, she preened over Micah.
His supple neck
lighter lined than Abe's
his unbent back ...
I caught Micah washing at the creek
more than once
watched the sun set fire to the water
coursing down his corded flesh
and it made me want
and wet down there
but his eyes, paler than Abe's
—like watered-down whiskey—
never reflected my flare, and I knew
he was not a man the whole way through.
Different women may be needing
different things.
By then I knew men do.
For someone like Saint Marguerite
I thought,
a fine view and a perfect kiss
might suffice, but the way she fussed
over his hands so smooth
his fingers clean and nimble...

My hands were always stained.
Marguerite's were thick as a man's
from shearing, knitting, and numbers
and Camille's danced like shape notes
ever braiding and unbraiding
her hair as she sang the flock
to pasture and back
but I was a mistress of color.
I seduced sepia from white birch
and scarlet from chokecherries.
I wooed cerulean from woad
and peridot from pigweed.

I wore my work like gloves
yet my gloved hands never failed
to work a man's magic.
Quite the contrary—
by constantly shedding colored disguise
my hands became quite sly.
One night I worked Abe thrice
and his wits came unwoven
his secrets unraveled
and he told me the truth.

Abe's Interlude

After several hours' crunching
our bed of cones and needles
we roped our shoes around our neck
and trekked into the river.
We slogged against its sawtooth current
embraced the numbness
spreading up our legs
—still only two then—
since it silenced our doubled soul
and staved off the weariness
that would not relent to sleep.

Only when the sun rose
did we see we were going east
and though that twist of river
angled upward, why, a lightness
lifted our shoulders!
It cracked open our chest
split our cloven soul.
And so strong was the sensation
of rising, of some weight shearing off
that we looked behind us
to see what we might've lost.

There was Micah,
as if our reflection had been
bullied back by the current.
But splashing, this shape fought
to keep pace with us.
We turned and struggled on
relieved to be divested of that one
who had yearned for the mine owner's son
(and others too, if truth be told).

He called to us to wait
but we crashed against the current
fists clenched, bare feet plunging
through the surface
into the second, sharper river
the colder one, deeper
that lurks within.
Another tap of the pick-axe
and a second weight slid free,
even as we, four-legged now
dredged up a third river.

We turned to see, not just Micah

and the soft silt we'd churned
into a current, but Connor too
(or three), lighter yet.
And who knows how many more
of us we might've jogged loose
had not that sight, as of
a fogged mirror cracked
shocked me so I spilled onto the verge
and Micah caught up with me
and Connor with him with me
and there we were, all three?
Six legs all'a sudden
but still not enough
to outrun our secret.

V. Connor

We never suspected three souls
hidden within our chest
but it seemed for the best
when we met the three sisters
with their limping-along sheep farm.
For we'd found no escape
from one another
—the pain of further separation
like a pick-axe to the skull—
and there was no re-fusing
—running west, with the currents,
always failed. So, much as Abe
wished to ditch Micah
and both of them estrange from me
we were three in one
one in three.

Camille was old enough to marry
but young enough to pale
at Abe and Adelita's passionate displays
naïve enough she didn't see
Micah and Marguerite's propriety
was its own display
akin to the way we played
house: our kisses little more
than bumped noses
our hands clasped rather than
our bodies, our baby
Adelita's.

I liked the sheep, who hovered
over the timothy grass like one

many-eyed, many-legged beast
attuned to the wind and Camille's songs.
Their ears flicked like shape notes
on a rustled page.
And I liked Camille, who corralled
the creatures with one song
set them free with another
who somehow harmonized
with herself, a choir of one.

Before we came, Camille pastured the sheep
with only her song, but after
she let me bring a shotgun
to warn off wandering dogs
the occasional coyote.
We'd saddle up a sheep for Dolly
another with our wrapped lunch
and set out for clover.
We'd return with the sun
chasing our long shadows to the door
and Camille's long braids
slapping her sturdy back.

When Micah went to town
to sell Adelita's bouquets of yarn
and Marguerite's knitting
we rode along, Camille and Dolly
jostling in the wagon.
While Micah attended to business
then vanished on "personal" errands
we lavished licorice and ribbon candy
on Dolly. We held her up to admire
the tinplate circus in the general store windows
held dresses up against
her wriggly body.

If Camille noticed
my headache-triggered temper
or Micah's mysterious new ease
on our journey home
she said nothing.
She sang though
the same harmony she used to weave
stray sheep into the flock
as she braided Dolly's
floss-fine hair.
More than once I wondered
if my relief truly came from reuniting
with Abe—who never smiled to see us—

or from Camille's gentle chorus
weaving our straggly family
together again.

One night before bed
Camille unwound her braids
by lamplight
and brushed her hair so long
it was like the locks had never
been separated, nor twisted
into trios. I worried what she was thinking
what weighty edict might lie
rope-ripe on her tongue
but then the sheep startled
and bleated and butted up against
the walls of their barn
till the wood creaked mutiny.

I rushed outside with shotgun
and Camille followed with lamp and song.
Micah and Marguerite soon joined us
Dolly in Micah's arms, and a rifle
in Marguerite's
and then Abe and Adelita
one gun and two blankets between them.
We lit more lamps and searched out
the threat, the sheep still thrashing
in their haven, but saw no sign
of bobcat or coyote, dog, fox or man.

While Camille soothed the flock
with arias of sleep and peace
we edged into the horizon
imagining wolves and notching guns
to tense shoulders. But nothing slunk
through the tall timothy grass or lurked
in tree-clumped shadows. The cicadas
and chorus frogs went silent
at nothing but our stomping feet.

We returned and Adelita grabbed Abe
with hands dyed whiskey-brown
from brewing goldenrod, and whipped him
down the path to their house
to finish their lusty fumbling.
Micah escorted wife and child indoors
but Camille lingered in the barn
still chanting at the nervous sheep.

I crept up and stroked the curtain
of hair from her face, asked her
to come inside. She turned into
my touch and asked
Was she a good wife?

VI. Camille

I'd long loved Connor.
First, for the kindness in his eyes
though they were strange
like un-aged whiskey, clear and bright.
Then, for the mercy he showed me
making no demands of a girl
not ready for the marriage bed.
For the lightness of his touch
with Dolly and all small creatures.
For the sweet, simple rest he took
in my arms, in my song
on wagon rides home.

I never understood his brothers' scorn
their jokes about his faded hair
his white lightning eyes
his wrinkleless neck and slight form
especially since his everything
differed in degree not form
from their own. Yet perhaps
his gentle humor wore them down
or my song worked its spell.
For finally
they stopped ribbing, stopped snubbing
and one day Dolly and I
back from gathering goldenrod
found the three brothers struggling
to free a fat ewe from the slats
of a paddock
and all three were covered in mud
and laughing so hard, their guts ached
longer than the bruises
from her cloven kicks.

Only, even as Micah and Abe
accepted Connor
my sister Adelita turned against him.
To my shame, I first suspected
that she, in a moment hotblooded
had gotten too close
perhaps touched him as she did Abe

or looked at him the way
she did Micah, early on.
I could imagine it; it pecked at my heart
even though I knew
honorable Connor would guard
her pride and mine.

Not till the night of the sheep's panic
did I understand. The stink of fear
twined in my hair that moments before
I'd brushed so long it shone, while
Connor explained that though he loved me
he could not love me
as Abe did Adelita.
His eyes welled
more water than whiskey
by my trembling lamplight
and his pale mouth tightened
unwilling to let loose
some feral, fanged secret.

With cheeks ripe as chokecherries
I wondered at myself:
How could I hope to evoke
the passion Adelita brewed,
I with my childish braids
and skittish heart?
So I conjured from the dark
a shadow of a smile
and I tucked myself beneath
Connor's gentle white arm.
I let him lead me
home.

But seeing our bed with the woad-
embroidered sheets, my heart split open
and I could not bear to lie
beside a brother rather than a lover.
So I twined my fingers in his and said
"I know I've clung to youth too long
and it's no wonder you think me
more little sister than wife
but can we try? Maybe you can love me
at least a little bit?
Like Micah and Marguerite?"

His fingers fisted around mine
and I thought his supple neck

had tensed with fury.
But before my shock slid to panic
he shook his head and said
"Micah does not love Marguerite
not as a husband does a wife.
He hides behind her skirts
and grateful, performs as best he can.
But her apron strings are still a noose
for one who loves other men."
As if reading shape notes
I grasped his sense
before I understood his words
and I trembled, anticipating
the next verse, but Connor struck
a chord I couldn't foresee
explained my husband
—in name though not in deed—
desired neither man
nor woman
felt no burning of that kind.
He only wished I'd be his single friend
the way he begged to be mine.

I couldn't speak, no more than
I could pull out the phantom needle
piercing my heart
or maybe it was a pick-axe
the way the pain
cracked open my chest.
All I could do was scrape
his hand from mine
and run.

I crashed into the woods like a blind beast
snapping twigs loud as a herd of
clumsy cloven feet and startling
the choral frogs into silence.
Wild sobs unwound from
my mouth, endless as the lies
woven to trap me in this life.

My sisters must've known
how Connor differed
yet still they let me cleave to him
thinking only how neatly
this knotted all their loose ends:
Abe to absolve Adelita's sins
Marguerite to harbor Micah

Connor, my consolation,
and three new backs, strong and unbent
to prop our struggling farm.
Did they never think I'd want
what they had?
They'd been as careless of me
as with Dolly.

Part of me slept there in the pines
and part of me raved through the night and dawn
and yet another part
grew hungrier in my belly than
between my legs, but I refused to rise
from the marsh of my tears.
Connor didn't come for me.
Abe did, a smile on his lips
chiseled from stronger stuff.
And true, after years of Adelita
he was wiser in the ways
of luring wild-eyed women
from the ledge of ultimatum.

He knelt beside me, stroked my hair
his words timed to the soothing
passes of his smooth hands
two shades darker than Connor's
two wishes warmer ...
"There, there, girl.
Don't cry no more.
Here's the morning and ain't nothing
we can't mend by its sweet light."
I twisted away and sobbed.
"Don't speak to me as if I'm Dolly
with a skinned knee. I'm married
to a man who can't love me
who can't bear to touch me
and you knew it, all of you."

Which was when Abe bent
and whispered near my ear
about knowing need
and what, if daring, we could do.

Micah's Interlude

Headache subsiding,
I sagged with relief
unseeing but knowing
Abe had returned, finally forfeiting

his wild-girl chase.
Camille had trudged home
near an hour before
and though she glared Connor into exile
—he slunk next door—
now she sucked honey and cornbread
from her fingers, while Marguerite
carded pine needles from her hair
and Dolly watched Adelita brew
walnut hulls for coal-black dye.

Abe opened the door and smote
one headache, only to ignite another.
I saw the sickened rage flare
from Camille's still-red eyes
and disgust pinched my lips,
mimicked Abe's mouth pursed
in silent threat.
I felt a fist in my throat, a stopper
of frustration fit to match
my clenched hands.
Abe's impulses: so pure and
sanctioned
and always pitching us
into thickets.

Saint Marguerite
by now well versed
as Dolly in let's pretend
was too engrossed in her carding work
to notice the storm surge
but Adelita …
her hands, drenched black
stopped stirring and she glanced
from Abe to Camille
and she understood his betrayal at once
verdict heavy
as a sledgehammer.

Camille fled
to the comfort of her sheep
or perhaps to comfort her sheep
for again they bleated and beat
their heads against the paddock
in unison: their wont whenever
unease ruffled Camille's spirit.
Abe and Adelita argued
with mouths more teeth than lips

and fewer words than kicks and fists.
Marguerite escaped under guise
of shielding Dolly from her parents' fury
but I, though not so fair as Connor
had fallen out of Adelita's sight
as well as favor
and Abe considered me
less than piss or shadow
so, ignored, I stayed and sipped
my coffee, let their repetition
drift me back
to old regrets.

The mine owner's son ...
did his daddy's money still pull
the punches of suspicious drunks?
Or had his whiskey-bright eyes
gone dull as the dust on a hanged man's
shoes? Had he found saint's rest
like me? Had he nothing left to lose?

VII. The Flock

The one called Adelita, she had black hands and a black web over her
heart that We have learned is called hate and is knit from bright barbed
wire (*vanity*) and begging, bloody wool (*hurt*). The Adelita threatened to
leave us and the songs We sang in the backs of our brains stopped, as still
as the chorus frogs when they sense the shadows with teeth and claws. For
long ago We were *separate*: some had arms and legs and eyes they called
their own and they wandered from the flock and were lost, only they
called it *freedom* and thought it sweet. But the Adelita was already lost,
had forgotten the binding song, and her threat was thunder drowning the
notes that shaped our flock.

In the Adelita's arms fought the small one, much loved by all, she
who rode with us and smelled of sticky ribbons and climbed the separate
arms and legs, and she was called Dolly for her smallness and how she
was passed around. The one called saint and Marguerite wept, which is
like rain but bitter, and the one called Micah reached for the Dolly, who
reached back. But the Adelita kept the Dolly trapped in arms like paddock
locks and howled what is Truth: that even longer ago, the many were one.
Only her hate-laced heart spoke to hurt not heal us, and this made the
one called Abe roar and run at the Adelita with hands clenched into fists,
which is a way of turning many into one also, but still to hurt not to heal.

Yes, it is awful all the things We did when We were not We but Them.

The one called Camille ran from the paddock and We followed her,
for even then We sensed her sameness and would be where she was.
We saw the Abe squeeze his fists around the Adelita's throat to stop the
words from coming out—words are broken bits of song that sink and

fall and sometimes pull the world down with them—and there was much screaming—which is words pushed past song and shattered. The Dolly, still in arms, she was not screaming but singing a song of gathering—she had learned the harmonies from the Camille—only her voice was small and the tune lonely and the separate ears would not hear.

Finally the one called Connor, beloved of Camille, he made a thicket of himself and pushed between the Adelita and the Abe. He fought to scrape fists from throat. But then the Dolly fell and there was a shattering inside her. The one called Camille shared the shattering and we ran to catch her on our huddled backs. But she did not fall, though her song fell silent under ache.

Our many hearts beat many notes. We were afraid.

Unknowing, the others rushed to lift the small one, while the Camille thought scarlet thoughts of things we did not understand, like *pick-axes* and *knitting needles, sledgehammers* and *shotguns*, until her ache gave way to screams. But, like ours, the Camille's throat was not formed for screams, and with our muzzles nudging, she quick pushed past the shattering inside her to sing a new song, a song of healing. Like the whispering of wind over clover, it had no words, only verses. But the song was round— *never leaving, never letting go*—and the chorus was *Forever*.

Connor's Epilogue

We are here. We are a part, apart. We remember no names but *Camille*. We have long loved Camille.

We will not say "in our own way." Love is the way.

We are some of us restless. Even now, we remember other bodies and make skirmishes in our self. But We are strong enough to break the bonds of wood and wire, broad enough to raze the meadows. Together, We are free.

There are other flocks who roam the valleys, and they look like us but they bolt from us for they are not like us. We carry a strange bouquet. We reek of coal and whiskey, licorice and lust, chokecherries and woad, wolf and rope and rust.

We age and die. We bear and grow. But our number is no matter. There is no *I* or *him, her* or *them*, me or you to know.

Sometimes the wind carries our song. We feel it on our muzzles and in our blood, looped through our wool, like a leash we've come to love. We can no longer sing, lyrics useless to our tongues, but we have no need: We *are* the song.

La Llorana

Margaret Randall

It should come as no surprise.
I found her
by the banks of the San Antonio.

I know, you'd think she'd choose
the Rio Grande or Colorado
for her nightly walks:
rivers of strength and purpose,
dividing nations or raging
through the greatest canyon of them all.
But I knew
she preferred more intimate beauty.
I'd done my homework.

I almost didn't hear her whispered wail
between the moan of freight trains
charging night
in that south Texas city.
I thought I discerned a minor key,
high harmony in late September
and followed the sound
notebook in hand,
sharpened pencil ready.

Around the bend she sat alone,
magnificent profile
hidden beneath her long black veil
I confused at first
with tree shadows in quiet air.
Almost midnight,
still high nineties.
Who could sleep?
I thought she might run
but she turned
slowly toward me,
seemed resigned to talk.

Gain her confidence: oral historian's trick
before sympathy heated my blood
and for one brief moment
I felt what she felt
so many centuries before.
Do you mind if I sit, I trembled,
and she gave me to understand
scorn is a lonely companion,
she'd like the company.
Even legends
endure mistaken identity.

Fearful she'd fade in this Texas heat
I opened with the questions
I knew my readers wanted answers to:

Were you poor but beautiful?
Rich but ugly?
Or did you embody some other mix
of class and magnetism?
Did he come from afar
or was he someone
you played with as a child? You know,
before the era's gender roles kept you apart?

And, I took a breath, *let's talk*
about the children
—I know it must still be painful—
but there's no getting around it,
people want to know.
Did you drown them yourself
or was it someone else
pinned the crime on you?
Their father? Some other authority?

I knew I was breaking every journalistic rule
of free-world impartiality,
feeding questions,
imposing twenty-first century assumption
on this seventeenth century woman
who raised one slender hand
and brushed her veil aside.
A full moon infused her copper skin.
Eyes I'd expected puffy and red
pierced mine.

You've got to understand, she began,
her voice the rustle
of a thousand sandhill cranes,
we had few choices when I was alive.
It was marriage
or spend the rest of your days
serving father and brothers.
And yes, she leaned forward,
her face almost touching mine,
the rancid stench of wet leaves

penetrating my nostrils
as I steadied notebook,
struggled to breathe,
why keep it a secret after all this time:
my sort of beauty wasn't praised—
large nose and ears,
a few extra pounds,

fuzzy shadow smudging my upper lip,
eyes that saw too much.
I wanted out ... no, no, erase that:
I had to escape or I'd have gone mad.

I know people say I was mad
but I was a woman with her life
and we didn't live long
back then,
one life I wasn't going to spend
with a man who only came home
tired of his latest fancy
and reeking of pulque,
how I recoiled at the sickening stench.

I loved my two little boys, of course I did,
Benjamín and Ceferino,
yes they had names
and I want you to name them,
all these years and no one's bothered to ask.
I loved my children and
I'll tell you now I tried to save them,
entered the river
though I couldn't swim,
struggled until water and reeds
threatened to pull me under,
watched the current carry their bodies away.

Why not proclaim my innocence?
I didn't expect that from you,
thought you smarter than to ask,
you must know we can talk and talk
and they still believe
only what fits the stories they write
to keep us under control.
Hysteric, they would have cried,
liar or worse.
Stories written long before my time
and I see nothing has changed that much.

Is that enough? She rose
and let the veil fall
across her dissolving face,
started to turn in resignation or disgust.
But maybe it was something in my eyes.
We were two women talking,
unperturbed by the distance
that separates her time from mine,

roles of historian and informant
long forgotten.

She offered one last smile
and I saw a glimmer
of sympathy
as if I was the twisted legend
and she the poet
destined to set the record straight.
Before she disappeared for good
among the oak and fruitless mahogany
she touched my hand.

Maybe in another hundred years, she said,
if our Mother hasn't devoured us all
and spit us back to space by then.

Enter Persephone

Marsheila Rockwell

A maiden
Fair as Aphrodite
Carefree as an unpursued nymph
Dances, unwitting
Across Demeter's pasture

•

She pirouettes
A silken dervish
Golden skin flashing
Laughter ringing out
Joyful, pleased
A siren call of innocence
To stir the loins
Of god and mortal alike

*

He'll hear
Demeter thinks
And with that thought
Grass begins to undulate
Roots burst forth from clutching soil
Meadowflesh rises up, hungry
Catching the unwary dancer
Mid-whirl

*

A frenzied moment
Then the greensward quiets
Returning to its slumber
Undisturbed now by step or song
Nothing to show the girl's passing
But a fresh
Flower-dotted barrow

*

Enter Persephone
Laughing, dancing
(Though neither so sweetly as the maiden)
Plucking hapless blooms
From the new meadow mound

*

As Demeter watches, hidden
The earth cracks open
Hades ascends in his terrible chariot
Snatches Persephone up
Unmindful of screams and futile fists
And carries her into the Underworld

*

The cleft closes
The meadow is silent once more
Save for one long
Slow
Sigh of relief

*

So a mother
Weary of motherhood
Gains a few moments of ambrosial respite
And the disapproving gods
Clucking behind their perfect hands
Nevertheless spread
The myth of maternal grief
For they know
If she breaks
The world breaks with her
And even Olympus might not be spared

*

Better a season of ruin
Than an eternity

Galatea

Mary A. Turzillo

In his mind, the artist sees the perfect woman,
more beautiful than any mortal eyes can compass,
a woman of the soul, daughter of dragons,
sister to the sea-nymphs, marble made flesh.
He would have no mortal bride.

He finds a likely lump of clay, a mud clod,
lying in his path, somehow seducing..
And in his mind begins creating.
His hands knead and shape, mind awakens mud.
He makes a woman. She is half alive.

An awkward thing, lisping and gawking,
clay feet and drooling mouth.
He can fix that. He is an artist.
He shapes her face, molds her breasts,
making out of dirt his perfect mistress.

He looks around at mortal women,
idealizes flesh he sees and gives it to his creature.
Now it is time to name this thing.
Shall she be Eliza? Shall he call her Dulcinea?
She can hardly speak, for he has not yet given her a soul.
But he calls her Galatea. Teaches her to speak her name.

She is formed of loveliness: he is a master sculptor
But it needs more. She needs the poet's touch.
He teaches her to talk, teaches her the words
the daughter of dragons, mistress of the night sky would speak.
He schools her, takes her to other artists,
makes her a lady. More than a lady,
a princess, a queen of the darkness inside clay,
an empress. A goddess. Galatea.

He teaches her to love, for mud does not know love.
He lights a brand from his own dragon soul
and gives that flame to her. She begins to glow.
Galatea, Galatea. And he falls in love,
because that was his point, to make a woman
resplendent, divine enough, to earn his love.

He takes her on his arm, his consort.
Others of his tribe behold and fall in love,
for she is all the splendor that the artist has within.
They look at her and see the artist's dragon soul.

Men fall in love with her because of what he made of her.

And she is vain. For he forgot to give her modesty.
Modesty seemed unneeded among virtues
for this perfect queen, this goddess.
She bestows her light on this and that one,
for she is capable of ardor, full of lust.
The perfect woman, naturally, is full of passion,
and the artist neglected fidelity among his gifts.

She scrutinizes him. He is imperfect. Human.
Why should she not have many worshipers?
Men fall at her feet, lick her hands, sport as if in rut,
and she entertains the ones who most flatter her.

Her fickleness hurts the artist. Why must she seek others?
Why does her eye wander? This man and that
catches her fancy; she disappears long months
with whatever dandy gives her gifts or flattery.
Then she returns. But the artist is broken.

She is his love. Her flame is his dragon flame.
How can she flit like a tawdry moth here and there?
And finally, because he didn't give her perfect vision,
she favors a toad-like man pushed at her by sycophants.
She sends the artist taunting letters.
She mocks his love, his art, his dragon soul.

And the artist falters. He stumbles and descends
into the pit his own art creates for him,
a hell made of his own imaginings.
It is the end. He dies a hero's death
battling imaginary trolls, phantasmal gryphons,
things of the same stuff of which he made Galatea,
monsters of his own creation.

Galatea, far and farther from her maker's flame,
loses the framework of her beauty.
Her features melt and drag; it is not so much age
as dissolution which deforms her beauty.
She hulks; she laughs ugly hawking gasps.
Her words fail her.
Soon she can no longer speak.

And then her eyes go muddy
and her profile blunts.
Her perfect figure slumps to bags of mud.
She dines on worms and toads,
and sometimes plays the whore with them.

And finally becomes the mud of which the artist made her.

As to him, the artist burns his dragon flame,
his eyes close, his lips are dumb,
he turns to charred oak, splintered marble, tempered steel.
Only his poetry and art speak for him,
speeches from beyond his grave.

His comrades sing his fate with bitter love.
Mortal woman grieve at his monument,
seeking the fire his dragon heart once held.
But he is cold,
and he will have no mortal bride.

Tohoku Tsunami

Mary A. Turzillo

Taro finds a sea turtle
belly-up, helpless, tormented by thugs:
he rights it, cradles, gives it back to the sea.

Another sea turtle, immense,
as from woodcuts of monsters devouring Kyoto,
walks out of the tide, finds Taro

dumbstruck, afraid.
But Fisherman Taro, doused with sea-spittle,
grows gills.

Come, come with me. The huge turtle
named Ryujin, sea kami,
tows him to ocean's root:

a palace refulgent
with kanju, chrysoberyls that make the tide fall.
and manju, alexandrine plates that make the tide rise.

The kanju are scales
the manju also
are scales.

The palace is a dragon.
In its deepest coil, Ryujin presents
Princess Otohime. *My daughter:*

the turtle you returned to the sea.
Otohime's beauty sponges away Taro's recall
of fishing and Miyagi, his home.

Taro, Otohime's consort now,
lives in a palace. It stirs now and then,
scales as chrysoprase, corundum, coils serpentine.

The dragon
Ryugoju, seabed, origin, center,
coils jealous around princess and fisher.

Taro yearns to see his mother.
Otohime (salt tears) agrees, gives him a box. *Do not open.*
He forgets to ask why.

The dragon
ready to sleep years, centuries, aeons,
releases Taro.

Taro walks inland,
finds Miyagi's streets
buzz with cars, light-blaze, women in brief skirts.

He asks
have you heard of Taro, the fisherman?
Urashima Taro? Yes.

A legend. Walked into the sea
to rescue a turtle. Never returned,
but his footprints on the beach were lined with jewels.

Taro asks of his mother.
That was long ago, they say.
She has been dead three centuries.

He sinks down.
All he knew is the dust of burnt offerings;
he is wayfarer in an arid, metallic land.

Bereft on a city curb,
he remembers the box
It will bring back my world.

He opens:
an echoing dragon sea-heart opens.
The dragon's jewel-scales flex. First the kanju,

call the sea back to the dragon
so the tide sinks,
and folk wonder has the sea abandoned us?

The dragon flexes again
and his belly-scale manju ripple
and the water rushes inland.

All is awash, lights put out,
temples cars people crushed
as an anthill engulfed

until finally the vat opens
where the folk grow electricity,
irradiating Miyagi

with billion-jellyfish poison
and, not having sea turtle shells,
folk tumble, sicken, and die.

The sea washes Taro back
to the palace-dragon,
which coils, then yawns.

The princess closes the box.
But no man
can live three hundred years.

Taro ages and fails, blood staining salt water. He dies.
The princess weeps.
The dragon, flood-weary, sleeps.

Carrington's Ferry

Mike Allen

What threat
could these scaly oarsmen ever pose?
She dodged Miró's famished halo
of animalcules, Picasso's rutting minotaur,
Tanguy's liquid, probing pebbles.
Deflected Dali's softening emissions.
Sidestepped Duchamp's fractured descent.
Her Cerberus grew far more heads
than most. She kept the one whose kiss
she chose to return, and killed
any others who rashly fought off sleep.
Compared to them, this boatful of lizards,
this hooded ferryman with forked tongue
has no hope in hell of harming her.

She looks back
at the red-gowned women,
the graceful petals of their heads,
pale orchid blooms, nodding
with the rhythm of the wind.

Will they warn her
if her next step goes awry?

She'd first glimpsed them in the English gardens
where she frolicked as a girl, but
they never spoke, offered no chat,
unlike the slow, thoughtful statues
or the stained glass peacocks who
would happily shriek her ears off—
Don't let them send you away, they pleaded,
Come back to us, come back to us.

How she tried, rebelled against her schoolmasters
whether at work or play, kept her attention
focused in other space, the space she meant to see.
How tight the sheets they wrapped her in
to trap her, drag her silent from the hedgerow maze.

No matter how shallow her footprints,
the thunderous black beast sniffed out her path,
the stone of her father's face crowning its shoulders,
battlements shielding his ears, eyes empty
as her hopes of escape. She would be a gift
to the King, a dainty mosaic mortared
in his courtyard, a bauble of fancied flesh.
She attempted epic quests, all the time
the tether-thread coiled around her wrist,
drawing her back to the drawing room.

Until the orchid maids nodded.

The tunnel to their altar opened in his chest,
this silver-haired, sly-smiling German,
rimmed with light, shaded with night,
the passage opening and opening into his
body and beyond, her thread redirected inside,
a guide to navigate a new labyrinth—
she left a chortling hyena in her ballroom clothes
and stole off to Paris, walked naked
past the all-consuming artists' eyes
and told that dirty Spaniard Miró
to fetch his own damn cigarettes.
Her Max, already wed; but he could not
and would not deny her.

And the demons
climbed from blood-soaked soil,
too many to resist, and pried him away;
laughing through dog fangs,

kicking with jackboots,
snarling with panther muzzles,
armored with Panzer hide,
running her down as she fled,
carrying her into the Spanish asylum
where they pinned her down and
racked her with volts, poisoned her brain,
ground against her bucking spirit,
quested to invade the maze, hunting
for the gate she desperately held shut.

Her father sent a rescuer by submarine
but as the taxi rushed the Lisbon streets
a voice heard from the wrong end
of a trumpet whispered new instructions
and she demanded instead the embassy
to Mexico—what chance Picasso's
startled friend would greet her there?
What chance, in the distance past his shoulder,
she'd see pale orchids nod their stately heads?

The Nazis could not reach her anymore,
nor the nouveau riche or the House of Lords.
The hero twins called on her, the hunter
and the jaguar, the grinning monkeys
and the serpent who gifted her
with feathers of every color,
fierce Frida and her monster Diego.
If she ever grew weary from their company,
she could always steal into the hedgerows,
her private garden where mannered harpies
poured tea and priestesses bowed their horns,
attendants in crow masks bathed exquisite vultures
and butterfly-winged sphinxes guarded their eggs
as Tarot trumps walked arm in arm,
witchy trinities mixed spells in flower cups
and faces peered from canopies,
playful ghosts snagged in the trees.
Asked where she birthed the wonders,
she snapped, You overthink. It's about
seeing, about visions into other space.
Both lands loved her in return.
For decades she dreamed, long since freed
of any limits.

Stone touched by her fingertips took flight.

•

In the maze, dark waters rise.

The orchid maids watch.
The ferrymen wait.
She snorts at them and turns
the other way.

She walks across the forest, looming
into the sky. The wheatstalks
of her hair channel the sun.

She unfastens her robes, exposes
hieroglyphs etched on her skin.
Birds spill from beneath her breasts,
shade the countryside with outstretched wings.

Capgras

Robert Borski

After dinner the charade
continued, with the imposter
who wasn't her husband
sitting across from her
pretending to take an interest
in the imaginary novel
that was now their seven years
of marriage together.

Apparently he'd been given
a new bunch of memories
to go along with everything
else (although the persistent
dirt under his fingernails
was not something *her* Tom
would have tolerated for long)
and was now giving them
a bit of a test drive.

*Hey, Rachel. Remember the one
and only time we made love
under the stars? We should
try that again sometime.*

Then again, if an exact physical
simulacrum could be deployed
right down to Tom's inverted nipples,
acne scars, and fingerprints,
certainly some method for harvesting
and encoding memories must also

have existed. Just plug them
into the motherboard and circuitry
of the brain. Wasn't there, in fact,
a modern zen parable about an old
car that had every one of its parts
gradually replaced, creating a new
bogus original?

Blah, blah, blah, said her husband,
the imposter, continuing with his polite
fiction, asking again about her day.
But why? Was it really that important
to maintain an illusion of domestic
tranquility between the two? What
would happen if word leaked out
that various partnerships were slowly
being infiltrated, replaced by near
exact duplicates?

Relax, darling, her mother would always
advise over martinis and brie. *Husbands
never turn out to be the men we married.
Even gays know this now.*

Nevertheless, online, she'd found
a support group of men and women
who all claimed the same thing—
that their spouses had been replaced
by carefully-nurtured imposters—
although follow-up commentary
by alleged "professionals" cited
over and over again some sort
of syndrome whose name she could
never quite remember—*crabgrass*
seemed close and at least had
a familiar context.

Perhaps women who married identical
twins fell into a similar sort of displacement
revelry, fantasizing, not about their well-
manicured lawn, but its wilder, rampaging,
sibling offshoot. Wouldn't it therefore be
easier, she often asked herself, to enjoy
the erotic doppelgänger aspect; the faux
infidelity of otherness?

Or, perhaps as her father had suggested,
she just resented Tom's new leisure.
Since he'd received his inheritance—

apparently, he was the favorite nephew
of an eccentric old aunt who collected
husbands and bank accounts,
but whose name had never quite come
up before—and quit his job,
he'd indulged himself in all sorts
of alternate interests.

Certainly, this year like never before,
the garden was flourishing. Out back
now — a post-prandial stroll Tom
insisted they make each evening
so he could tout his horticultural progress—
they made their way between huge sacks
of Miracle-Gro and giant mounds
of compost to the rows of exotic
green that comprised his latest
project: Asian pole beans, with pods
as big as bananas, and leaves
the size of pillows.

But even as she stood staring drowsily
at them, waiting for Tom to hand her
the inevitable sample,

she already could tell they would taste
like nothing out of this world—just as,
once upon a time, pre-displacement,
had his torrid unersatz kisses.

In the Beginning Was the Dish
Robert Borski

Not just saints or artists
are prone to revelation;
for those with the proper temperment,
and the patience to look, patterns,
however ordinary or prosaic the canvas,
can be divined everywhere:
in dried smears of catsup;
the burnt faces of grilled cheese;
the pale yellow masa
of tortilla shells; even the melting
evanescent scrim of ice cream
and chocolate syrup.

The onus for the seer, however,

is always to characterize such
revelations properly, to interpret
the Delphic calculus.

Some, if not most, will see images
of the Divine; the bearded son of
Yahweh or his weeping mother; Ganesh
flailing his trunks of curry; Buddha
transcending the tandoori of Indian
takeout (only a fool would fail to recognize
the parochial element in such "miraculous"
happenstance.) But truth to tell, such
misapprehensions are often the result
of what psychologists call pareidolia—
the ascribing of patterns to sheer randomness.

Unfortunately, caught up in their own
search for meaning, not even

the disciples of Freud recognize
the true cuneiform of food.
At least not as potently as I, nor
with as much reverence for
the actual artifacts, none of which
I eat or sell on eBay, but rather
collect each day, every secret
message a codex of scripts
no less perishable
than the Dead Sea scrolls, and which
I carry back to my current bivouac
at the Salvation Army.

If my understanding is correct
(and I will be the first to admit
my translations are but rudimentary
and inchoate), I am to be
the chronicler of what is soon to come;
the invasion's proto-evangelist
and first true believer. Sergeant Hobart,
as I'm called back-of-the-house
at the restaurant which employs me:
the pot-washing visionary.

Meanwhile, though hungry,
only after the ships have landed
and order's restored, will I allow
myself to eat. Soon, I hope—
for I intend to gorge myself
on scripture and dish soap.

Between the Mountain and the Moon

For Izlinda Hani Jamaluddin

Rose Lemberg

They say that in the oldest of times, the moon was always full; and sometimes she walked the world, changing shape as she would, and taught some others to do so.

Movement the First: Transformed

[The Black Panther]:
Out of my sisters I alone was born unspotted
under my mother's golden pelt, night-bodied in her warmth.
She nuzzled me away. Alone, I curdled on winter branches,
wrapped myself in the hunt. Birthed silence with each breath.

Day after day the mountain skewered the water
falling earthways, and the snow like milk
melted sharp under my tongue.

I hunted the spotted doe of the moon,
followed her on mothersoft paws.
Unseen, even in dreams—
only the moon saw me
quick-quick as she darted through the raingrass away.
I danced the sky on her smell-threads,
trusting the trees to catch my fall.

[The Moon]:
She leaps the cloudwood to me,
pelt as softest dark between
breath and another breath—
she dreams she hunts me through that emptiness
where young winds wrestle, where the grass grows tall
above the mountain. I have seen a house
          under its sleeping shadow, where a mother
weary from stillbirths, waits each night
with love like milk.

Listen, lithe child, little child
night-in-the-night-child—
once a winter pine wept on my sleeves,
once a black walnut wept on my shoulder.
I'll dip these needles into ink:
hush, lissome, I'll write you a skin-story,
I'll teach you a girl-shape,
tell you into a mother's orphaned house.

Movement the Second: Duet with Moon and Mountain
1.

[The Girl]:
At the gate, lanterns moan
under the limber fingers of the wind. Mother comes out quilt-warm
with a pail of milk, and her eyes
like the serving-women's, carefully averted.

No, I will not go in, clothe
in your padded garments, or veil
this needle-traced skin. I care not that young men
never ask for me, that pines tilt away,
that even the wind shuns me—

the spotted cat of the moon
my sistersoft leopardess
curls nightlong by my side, murmurs
hunt stories.

In this season of bleached bone
we'll chase snowrat and cloudhare,
claw the black mountain frost
for the sleeping frogs of the stars.

[The Suitor]:
Ah, this gate. The northeast wind has long peeled
its bashful paint away, pressed
caress after wild caress into the surrendering flesh of the wood.
Some nights, the groaning
shames the people in. Pretending decency,
they splash boiling river into clay; heads tilted
ever so politely to the east, they stir their tea
and veil the windows with seed-embroidered cloth.

Nothing like this ever lasts.

But lately, a young woman
comes out to the gate alone, undaunted
by the wind's lovemaking.
She lifts her storyspelled face, and her hair
falls back like a moan of night.

Listen, girl-woman,
shining woman, still woman,
skinwild woman, dreaming-fast woman—
I will go in, where they keep fire captive
in the deceitful embrace of glazed brick.
I will gift

garnet and oystershell to your kinswomen
and ask for their unmarriageable daughter.

2.

> [Girl:]
> *Sometimes at night, when every stone in slumber*
> *and every tree is pacified in matted frost*
> *breathed out by starlight, I am waking;*
> *uncoiling self to spotted moon,*
> *I muscle in the beast inside;*
> *between the clouds we curl together*
> *until she melts into the dawn*
> *and I, into this flesh*

[Suitor:]
Down by the mirrorlake they comb
my wild-grass hair with pearl and abalone; on the slopes
they gift me with garnet to flicker around my waist
  where tiger and mountain cat, deer and wild hare
    adorn my coat. And only in this town
they had forgotten about me, for while I slept
  they thought themselves safe from obligation.
Yet now that I wake, I do not rage
  at their foolish moth-fluttering lives,
    for she has snarled in my shadow.

Oh, I've been waiting for long years, polished my sleeves against the night;
Counting bloodbeats, shaman-hands against the earthskin of my ribs.
Play me, flowering dark—I long to be released
from your embrace,
and flood the heart of my beloved.

Movement the Third: At the Fire Festival

On the evening the starcounters have predicted a lunar eclipse, people
come together under the burgeoning moon; dressed in garments of burnt
umber and roped with cinnabar, they carry tigerlily torches and revel to
the sounds of iron drums as the drum of the sky is devoured by shadow.
It is said that at the Fire Festival one meets one's true love, or else is swept
by the sleeve of death.

> [Mother]: dancers   *arrogantly young*
> in spring's best, and this my child *sewed nothing*
>   in my late sister's garment. Still, it becomes her—
>   seed-embroidery over indigo
>   almost as dark as her eyes. *Is it in my womb*
> *that she was decorated so? What invisible fire*
> *reached into me and danced over her features,*

leaving this bitter char in its wake?
　　Here, at the fire festival
　　torches bloom; girls, twirling like gadfly wings,
sweep firecloth against the sweetness of pipe and percussion.
　　Every girl　*how I wish I was young still*
　　followed by suitors springing everywhere like moths from larvae.
　　　Is he coming for her　*that worthless*
　　　　belted in seed garnet *like he said*
　　arrogant in grass-wool　　*his eyes like opals*
　　　and each sleeve　*conceals a knife*
　　　and each sleeve sails over the air like stringed bow,
　　　voice　*treacherous*
　　　　like the voice of the ironframe drum—
　　　this one should be right for my daughter,
　　　　I often wonder how she's mine.

　[Girl:] oh spotted maiden, mirrored in every river
　　　beloved huntress, laughing over each glade—
　　come, pluck me from this pinwheel of suffocating light
　　　from the whirligig of steps to the smell of reed and blood,
　　to where there is only silence.

　　And if you are gone,
my heart will refuse its drumming.
　I will chase spirit-deer in the forests of regret
　　I will leap over the antlers of ash-trees, follow the scent
　　　of the bone-birch and the marrow-maple;
　　　　hunt—where there is no moon—
　　that shadow-hunter who pursues me.
　He comes from the mountain
in the cold of the night, when I am alone; measures
each of my breaths with his fireweed eyes.

　　　Fire.
　　I look up and see
　　　a roaring through the clotted veins of the sky
　　　has swallowed the forests.

　Life-destroyer, in my veins
　　your blood is home,
　　　your blood is like my own.
　　　　Your blood is me—and she is not with me,
　　　　　if she is not with me, where shall I go?

　He comes, he comes in coal-embroidered red
　　　roiling from the slopes in woven smoke and ash
　　　to dance the firedance in this ghostbone town
　　　　to dance the firedance with me, or with no-one.

No, mother. Flee if you want,
　　　　Flee if you want, but I will stay here.

Coda

They say that the moon descended to the burning town in the shape
of a golden leopard, and where she stepped, the lava turned into cold
black glass; and some say she came as a maiden, her amber face tattooed
with moon-circles, her eyes as dark as winter blood. Dressed only in her
starwoven hair she walked unafraid, looking for the one in whose voice
the ghosts of reedpipes still whispered, whose heartbeat echoed in the
melted iron of the drum—

　　　　the black leopardess
　　　　with pearls of black under her fur

No people remained there to witness, but when they returned with incense
and woven offerings to rebuild the town again in winter-hardened stone,
she came to them often in dreams

　　　　as soft as breath—you see her curled against her lover's shining
　　　　　　and growing fatter from the hunt each night
　　　　　　above the mountain

Black against yellow they make the moon together, casting their long
silences into the mirrorlake below like fishing lines after the fallen autumn
leaves. And when the moon is new, the spotted maiden walks the world
unseen to teach her word-music to those who can hear it;

　　　　and where lake is pearl, and deer and mountain-cat
　　　　are moonstone slivers in his wild-grass hair
　　　　　　when moon is full,
　　　　the black leopardess leaps down
　　　　　　to prowl his slopes as night is long,
　　　　　　　　to whisper to him as the night is long.

Came the Rogue

Sally Rosen Kindred

with excerpts from "The Wolf and the Seven Little Goats," Grimm's Fairy Tales,
trans. by Lucy Crane

1

*And now came the rogue the third time to the door and knocked. 'Open,
children!' cried he. 'Your dear mother has come home, and brought you each
something from the wood.'*

Mother
we've wanted   we've wanted
the third time we need

to believe you. The taste
of your paws white
with meal

on our cracked lips
with milk   on our lips
on our paws as we slept

Your touch not the rogue   not the rogue
and with gifts, your voice
chalk-soft and licking

its curtain, tongue-brown coming down

                    We want
to open. We want to open
for dear   your warm fur

you, gift
from the wood.

Came the rogue   Came the rogue

in your heft
in your breath   with your gifts
and what can you be

but a wolf

only a season   brute as ash
could make our bodies
this story

2

*When he was inside they saw it was the wolf, and they were terrified and
tried to hide themselves.*

Into the oven, into the clock-case,
up to the far black shelf
on cane
chairs that crack
their legs beneath ours

a waste, rearing our thin bones back
our skins bleat, we cry
away, our haste the blood-metal taste

of how lost

3

'Here I am, mother,' a little voice cried, 'here, in the clockcase.'

Survival. Tastes like heart-
wood ticking that rocks the body.
Tastes like gristle of clock in the teeth. Here I
am, mother. O
Mother, here I
                survive
my brothers, those softer
swallowed. The wood walls
of my body sorry me
home
shaking hands
big and little circling

over a face. Here I am again
wanting you
behind a door.

4

*'Now fetch some good hard stones,' said the mother, 'and we will fill his body
with them, as he lies asleep.'*

While you were gone
we learned to be stones

we learned inside the wolf
the fever-dark you pulled us from

In the sun again   we roll down
for the stream, unafraid to drown

hard and good
we make a fair trade

We are not sons
we are stones

we steam
where his bile stripped our names

though we can stand
and touch our lips   to your face we can't

believe. Mother, we hunker. We are
changed: our hunger

bright sky, a blue door
that hides you.

We curl under and smell
torn fur, our granite skin

still burning.

Quince

Samantha Henderson

I miss
the hypodermic benediction
that brought dreamless sleep.
These dreams I can't control; they are
       jagged,
              disordered
as a pack of shuffled cards, or the spill of textured bearings
into red dust.

Three miles above the surface, hills and hillocks and dunes
and the concentric volcanoes,
all layered and caked with fine, sunset grit,
take on the aspect of the rippled surface of an ancient marble
that an old man brought for luck
tucked in the flap of a utility suit. Like a stone peach,
in a stone bowl in a painting
in a book on a digi-drive.

Alarums. Acquire target: peck
pow
a burst of silent gravel
like a fruiting body
out of an ant's head.
Alarums. Acquire target: peck
pow

At home we eat oranges against the scurvy,
and apples mealy from the heat.
Sometimes there are grapes, each an explosion
of pallid juice, but sweet, a little, enough.

But here, I can revel in the memory of fruits never tasted
when the interface lulls me back into that place
between wake and sleep
between targets and the jagged dreams.
Quince, syrupy and pale yellow,

greengages ripe at fair-time
kumquats sweet and gloriously bitter
blood oranges tangy and clotted
apricots seasoned as wine, musky as sex—
the fruits are not necessary,
only their names.

One target, just one
can will wipe out a pod
just one can hit the nexus of tube and rivet
and all burst forth like a drop of blood
blooming in water.

They say that when you are tempted to let one, just one, pass
just to see what will happen—then it's time to go home,
to leave your catamites and concubines,
your tagger-girls and twilight-boys
the crimes uncommitted you savored
the sins you pretended to taste.

This time,
I'm keeping the quince.

Augury

Sandra Kasturi

Let us go into the augur
into his auguration
his divinity and divination
the lessons of augury
the lessons of august
gentlemen, of St. Augustine
and Augustinians, tall and short
Augustinians, truthsayers
and soothsayers
finding omens in the dust,
the bird-tracks of the future,
the switchback trails of truth
and memory, the tracks and tropes
of auk and auklet,
the ticklishness of their feathers,
the tricksiness of their hearts.
These are the lessons of augury.

Let us go into the past, into the aul
and the aula, let us sit there and learn
thick Teutonic languages,

the languages of augurs, in fact,
languages with g's and p's
and terrible r's, languages too
rough for birds, who only speak
auld romances like French
and Italian, the commedia dell'arte
of linguistics, liquid, languid,
measured in aums in aumailed cups,
like the fruits of augury, distilled
and mashed, pulped into sheets,
scripted and scribbled by augurs
and laid away in some dark aumbry
or the aumônières of dark Augustinians
who keep their secrets in their vests
and their lives in their little fingers,
a severed index of small sins, an auncel,
an aune, a French measure of samite,
a soupçon of sameness.

Let us get down to the last details,
au pied de la lettre, down
to the Augustinians, the auks
and auklets, their terrible auras
of extinction, glowing down
through the ages, their aureate crests
pressed in books of unnatural curiosities,
their sufferings pinned by aurelians
who do not differentiate between
priests and puffins.

Let us dispense with the Augustinians,
then, those august gentlemen. Let us dispense
with auks and auklets and their kin
and kind. Let us keep only these:
bird bones and finger bones and small
sins; languages without p's and g's
and growling r's. Keep the augurs,
and their auguries, but only on Sundays.
Keep the cups and the weights
and the measures. Keep the keeping of things,
the nearness of things, keep the keepers in fact.
And the far past, and the near past.
And the rewritten past. Yes, keep that too.

Snow by Gaslight

Sandra Kasturi

No kinder face does gaslight turn
than toward snow, new
with the smell of anticipated
Christmas, kitten-soft
and unmarked by little match girls
or fauns trotting back home
with their brown-wrapped parcels.

What kinder touch than the diffused tender glow
of an unexpected lamppost—found
in a snowy wood creeping toward that darkness
where even the few remaining sparrows,
deaf to the call of Capistrano, become
still, hushed to drowse of falling flakes
and gleaming shadows.

Even the prickle of holly and ivy
is smoothed away, enchanted,
lulled to silence, as the drifts blanket
and embrace each sharp Victorian house,
brittle with bric-a-brac and manners,
now creaking under the weight
of new, clean promises.

The quiet glow of gaslight that brings safety
and sleep, more than darkness ever did,
spreads throughout the globe—the clean
reflection of fallen snow quieting
the clock-mice, muffling the tarantella
of sugarplums and church bells,
gentling the grinchiest of hearts,
and softening even the most restless
of graveyards into a downy, dreaming settle.

Look, in the white-fronted, black-shuttered
dollhouse: the dolls themselves
have dozed off in front of the red paper
fire and painted lamps, knowing
the snow, at least, is real, and smoothes
and soothes and covers the house
that covers the house that covers them.

Watch! those of you who are half-asleep
and thick with enchantment—
as each Christmas tree grows taller

and taller, until small girls in white nightdresses
may creep step by step down stairs
and past stockings, down below
the great evergreen boughs, to see wooden prince
and seven-headed mouse king fight to an end
that is never really death, but only breaking of a spell.

Such gaslit snow comes but once
in your lifetime, in your memory,
drifting ivory from pages of lions,
of wardrobes and witches,
ghosts from holidays past and future, reindeer
and toymakers and wild geese and every
round moon that ever looked down upon
a snowbound lamppost and called it cousin,
friend, conspirator in silence.

Casting the Future
Serena Fusek

The artist dreams of them on a night of dark moon. She sees her hands
turning over the cards, glimpses the images.

She rises into a morning of yellow haze, the TV droning pollution alerts
and the latest update on the spreading oil spill. She pours a glass of pure
water, goes into her studio.

The first card she brings out of her dream is the Queen of Jaguars with
her roseate skin and golden eyes. She works without hesitation, without
redrawing a single line, as if in a trance.

The second painting is of the King of Ravens, a man with black hair and
feathered sleeves. At noon Crow Woman clamors for her depiction but the
artist's weary body drags itself into the kitchen and finally breaks her fast.

Outside her apartment window the city grinds on: traffic, crime, streets a
moving tide of humanity, several leashed to dogs. A few stunted trees grow
in cement planters but are drying up in the drought. No one considers
them important enough to water.

Crow Woman has mischief in her yellow eyes. Antlers grow from the hair
of the King of Deer. The Doe Mother leads her fawn or a lost soul through
the Suit of the Forest. The Salmon King knows the secrets of the Suit of
Water, both ocean and river. Grief clouds his human eyes.

From the website where the images first appear, it is the Salmon King who
is most often downloaded.

The Queen of Vultures, the King of Condors can use even what is spoiled. They ride the Suit of Storms: thunder, lightning, hurricanes, the undertaker wind, blizzard and forest fire.

The last cards created are the Suit of Youth, also called the Suit of Hope: children in nests, cubs in cradles, fledglings and kittens sleeping together on a pillow.

The decks are printed without a book of interpretation, but they are snatched up as soon as they appear. In the cards people see not fantasy or a dream but a reality that was hidden from them. From laminated cardboard that reality stares at them like a reflection in a mirror.

Sometimes the cards seem to move in the hands laying them out, like an animal stretching. Sometimes the Jaguar Queen looks straight at whoever is studying her. Blink and she is just a picture, but the nerves thrum from the recognition. The Suit of Youth revives dreams almost forgotten.

Someone starts to water the container trees. That is the first sign.

In cities of cement and steel, in glass towers in the sky, people lay out the cards and the spirit of the forest, of air and water enter the rooms.

In a woman on the subway, riders recognize the Jaguar Queen, the power and smell of the cat on her golden skin. The Prince of Wolves gleams from a young man's eyes.

In a year, in two, green breaks through the sidewalks. Deer browse in the parks. The trees break their pots, sink their roots through concrete into the earth and birds sing in every branch.

Mushroom Barley Soup: An Invocation
For Esther Smolowitz, 1914-1989

Shira Lipkin

When I curse, my profanity sours the broth.

I can't be too careful—
years of trial and error,
singing like my grandmother,
tripping forth the same mondegreen
(even though I know the lyrics)—
searching for the magic combination
that makes the food *hers*
makes it *right*
makes it *home.*

Each time, the ritual grows more elaborate,

complex—
her apron
the way her socks drooped
the hum behind her words
all of it hall-of-mirrors duplicated
down the years and down the kitchens
until I feel her,
just a wisp,
standing beside me,
stirring
nodding
sprinkling the salt.

Old magic
food magic
grandmother magic.

I try everything—
maybe it's the bowl,
green Depression glass
it's not her soup without it—
I try leaning as she did,
toward the end,
speaking half-nonsense
in the Yiddish she hardly knew.
She was born here,
learned from grandparents,
a smattering a scattering
good American girls don't—

I let slip a modernism.
She slips away.

I restart the ritual.
Wooden spoon
sensible shoes
slow-chopped mushrooms
singing singing
hesitate—there—
and I feel her creeping back.

She was not much taller than me.
Gnarled like friendly old trees
by the time I knew her;
never moved without pain.
I must be slow,
be patient.

My grandfather died when I was ten;

she never made the soup again.

The Clock House

Sonya Taaffe

*Be kind, resourceful, beautiful, friendly, have initiative, have a sense of humour,
tell right from wrong, make mistakes, fall in love, enjoy strawberries and cream …
do something really new.*

—Alan Turing, "Computing Machinery and Intelligence" (1950)

Come ghost out of the machine, Christopher,
the clouds are gathering in Cheshire and Aquila
and beyond the darkening lens
the last of the boy-martyrs are being put to bed
with a glass of milk and an apple,
immaculate faces sweetly sleeping out
wars, plagues, apologies.
Here is Prospero of the decision problem
who drowned his books in cyanide
and his wanly smiling Ariel,
long freed from the equivocations of flesh,
the absent-minded atheist and his good angel
haloed with the sun in hindsight
over Canal Street and a saint's blue shoulder—
Christopher, as if you never fought
or fucked in Alan's muddled, book-racked room
between the bicycle clips and the chess notations,
Ravel's concerto crackling on the 78
that late, wet spring of '32.
You took Wittgenstein's classes and a double First
and wrote of numbers as real as identities,
irrational, integral and complex,
a light-lashed theorist with a dark, diffident glance,
not talking of night gasps or sunlit, starch-white beds.
He was your runner, bearing back like laurels
the hot smudge of lakeland heather
or the breakneck shiver of Sark's summer waves,
your pillow book of the night-lit ward,
reading his dark hair with sweating fingers
until your fever broke and no one's heart with it.
He sent punch-cards for postcards,
his war work as vague
as yours was a simple arithmetic
of empty seats and chalk-cold afternoons,
the endless subtracting of Cambridge,
stained glass, coal, and undergraduates.

You thieved his tea-mug
off its chain each time, a pair of profs
to choose between—the thin twist of wrists
like piano wire, a static crackle of a laugh—
unbreakable cipher and key of Dilly's Grecian eye.
Your parents met him at the graveside,
hatless and mannerless, an old page of fixed stars
fisted in his pocket like a ring.
Your daughters met him on Market Street,
their shabby, alchemical half-uncle
who bought them ice-creams
and told them the story of *Snow White*
and maybe still, long before you, died.
This is where you disappear, Christopher,
the vanishing point Alan ran to
as his program was pulled from its tapes.
What can I construe from a letter, a photograph?
The body is safe as glass houses,
the mind a black box.
I can smash these screens, but I cannot know you
any more than a message from the unseen world—
the dead who are noise and incalculable
and memory the most passing machine of all,
Christopher, unless you come to tell me
of a slow twilight on the Cam, of two voices talking drowsily
of Delphinus and von Neumann, central limits, cinema,
saying *no, but look here,* meaning love.

The Necromantic Wine

Wade German

Where wattled dragons redly gape, that guard
A cowled magician peering on the damned
Thro' vials wherein a splendid poison burns.

—George Sterling

In simultaneous ruin, all my dreams
Fall like a rack of fuming vapors raised
To semblance by a necromant, and leave
Spirit and sense unthinkably alone
Above a universe of shrouded stars.

—Clark Ashton Smith

The blood-red sun begins its slow descent
Behind the distant, jagged line of peaks.
From this clear vantage on the flagstone roof
Where I have made a final hermitage
Of this abandoned tower in deep woods,
I watch those giant granite faces turn

From shades of grey to shade of cobalt blue;
And there above them, gliding on great wings,
I see the silver dragons in their flight
Returning to their eyries and high keeps.
The cool autumnal winds around me gust,
And now about me whirls a weirder breeze
Which whispers in my ear a rhyming rune—
And so an elemental speaks to me
Of her day's wanderings across the world,
And up into our planet's airless zones
That limited her flight to view the stars
Behind the vault of deep cerulean.
And now the wind grows wilder; she departs
To seek ethereal games with her own kind,
Amongst the changeling colors of the clouds
Aflame in twilight's final renderings.
The air grows cooler; so I step inside
And settle in beside the flame-fed hearth
To warm my bones, and smoke my briar pipe;
And lounging in narcotic quietude
I sip pale yellow wine and contemplate
The subtle incantations of the night.
But mortal issues rise to cloud my thought,
The same grey ghost that lately haunts the nights
Of this, my ancient age by sorcery
Sustained so many years beyond its span:
It seems I have grown weary of the world.
In youth, pursuit of wisdom was my quest,
And wonder, that bright star, had served as guide;
But somewhere in the passing centuries
Its incandescence dwindled; nearly dead,
That fulgent glow of wonder has gone out.
With what to stir the embers just a bit?
Despite the learning of three hundred years,
I never have held counsel with the dead;
I have but theories anyone might have
Of death's dimension and what lies beyond.
Ancestral imprecations on black arts
Have kept my line from straying to that gate;
But lately, I have pondered that old pact,
For there are other ways to gain the roads
Which dark magicians tread to seek strange truths;
I need not raise a corpse from its repose
By crude reanimation, or invoke
The wraiths who linger at unquiet graves;
I need not deal with ghouls in catacombs
Who sup on foul corruption in the crypt,

Nor need I bow to idols of dark gods.
Such methods—so impious and perverse!
There is a rarer magic, more refined
And suited to an acolyte of taste
Who would not risk an old familial curse ...
I once discovered in a desert tomb
Strange hieroglyphs engraved upon a stone
That mentioned of a necromantic wine:
A darkling, ruby wine of philtered spells
Distilled in huge alembics of a dream
A demigod once dreamt who, dying, spilled
The poison in a glass canopic jar
Attendant demons slew each other for.
Another mention of the wine is here,
In this Lemurian scroll: it is described
As wine both sweet and bitter to the tongue,
With mystic operations on the mind
Inscribing arcane words of alchemy.
In one grimoire, the potion is compared
To green absinthe—pale opalescent drops
Evolving in the poet-prophet's brow
A third eye blazing like a demon star
That sees behind occulted nature's veil.
And one old libram notes the legend well,
But states the ruby potion is composed
Of substances abused by oracles:
The pollen of black loti thrice refined
And alkaloids from flowers of the moon,
Affording hypnagogic properties
On those who seek to see the dead in dreams.
And such I know of necromantic wine.
Who knows for sure what wisdom it imparts?
I have a bottle here; there is one thing
Betwixt this rare elixir's spell and me:
The cork.
                    A darkness washes over me
Mere moments after sipping from the glass.
I shudder as a mist invades my mind,
The potion working like an anodyne.
My pulse throbs slowly, thudding as in sleep;
A sense of distance gathers in my head:
The chamber walls and ceiling now withdraw,
And all the candles glimmer distantly
Like witchlights in a black expanding pool.
I feel my body sink into the couch
And feel its fabric fray and then dissolve;
My atoms scatter as a thing destroyed.

Thus disembodied, and by wraith winds borne,
I am conveyed across the gulfs of night
And outer voids of undimensioned space
As swift hallucinations pass me by,
Successive strange horizons which unfold
Like tapestries, their imagery arrayed
In vast prismatic patterns which reveal
The surfaces of endless unknown worlds:
Strange vales and vistas, alien terrenes
With protean shores awash in pulsing hues,
The spans of all their suns and pendant moons.
But now the swarming throng of orbs disperse
And vanish out beyond my vision's reach
To merge with infinite immensities.
Now, in a region of black space, I see
A planet out of chaos newly formed:
Enormous storms that feed electric bale
Sweep red primordial skies with raving winds
As climates alternate in swift extremes.
Below the raging upper atmosphere,
Volcanoes bleed with endless lava flows,
And crimson rivers web a rifted main
Which quakes in primal night devoid of life.
And as the orb around its sun revolves,
Its smoking cauldron surface stills and cools,
And on it protoplasmic ichor gels:
Amoebic life-forms mindlessly evolve
And multiply at blind malignant rate—
The ancestors that spawn a fledgling race
Which treads across the dawns of centuries—
I see imperiums arise in time
And just as swiftly, witness their declines
By mode of nature or by work of man—
The cities lie collapsed in sunken seas
Or buried in abyssals of black sand;
The landscape quickly molders and decays;
The orb is now a planetary tomb
Where only subtle shadows faintly flit
Among the shrines and toppled monuments.
Again the vision fades. All sense deranged,
I hurtle through the interstellar deeps
And pass through regions of galactic cloud
Where I behold vast nurseries of stars
Which gleam like hellish rubies, xanthics, pearls
And fiery opals blazing into birth;
Then further, on accelerated course
Through unlit oceans of the outer dark

Until my flight decelerates in zones
Where Time's great gears have shuddered to a halt.
I stand upon the rim of the unknown.
Below me swirls a strange, phantasmal sea
In which converge wild raving cosmic streams
That gutter in fantastic cataracts
To feed the swirling whirlpool-gulfs below.
As if supplied by black ensorcelled lamps,
A weird dark radiance illumines all;
And from the gulf, huge shadow-things arise—
Twin ebon-bodied winged leviathans
With twisted limbs and long colossal claws.
They gather up dark matter in the gloom,
And from that substance, raise a massive gate
By thaumaturgic gestures. From its arch
Weird vortices of ectoplasm pour,
And in the gyrings, shapes of varied race
Rise up and multiply in manifold
Familiar shade—or take far stranger forms
Phantasmagoric, as in fever dream:
Of Titans, giants, gnomish folk, and imps,
And goblin beings, gargoyle-headed men;
And centaurs side-by-side with saurians,
Scale-tailed and crystal-eyed, in phantom ways;
And white arachnids, weirdly humanoid,
Which stride in spectral unison with things
Emerged from some mad god's menagerie—
Pale, luminescent algaes, many-eyed,
And faceless fungoid creatures, webbed and winged;
Odd floating orbs of psychic energy,
And other fabled forms innumerable,
Of otherworldly, unknown origins.
Now one thin wraith among the spectral throng—
Who is the only sample of his race—
Drifts forward as their sole ambassador,
And though he has no mouth with which to speak
I understand his language in my mind:
"We come in wonder, awe, and in our woe,
In death united and our knowledge pooled
(For what a shade has known all shades now know)
That one upon our portal is alive
Who treaded stars to seek our nebula:
Among our legions are the kings and queens,
The viziers, priests and wizards, generals
Of dynasties long dead, which ruled in realms
On planets orbiting the million suns
Your almagests and testaments assign

As white Subhel, and golden Azimech,
Blue Algol, and pale rose Aldebaran;
As orange Fomalhaut and Betelgeuse,
And Cabalatrab, red and emerald green;
And Genib, Iclil, Menkar, Deneb, Thuban,
Zedaron, Zaurak, Zubenelgenubi:
The alphas, betas, gammas in your charts
Which form the signs and symbols of the night,
The iconography of zodiacs.
The merfolk who once lived in cities spread
Beneath eternal vaults of lunar ice;
The globe-like beings of gas giant worlds
Who dwelled and drifted in pacific zones
Of atmosphere which like a cauldron brewed
Huge brooding storms that gathered gloom and churned
With centuries of crimson turbulence.
And others of an ever-changing shape
(For their true form is formlessness itself)
Who mimic those with whom they would converse;
And those who once inhabited no world
But flourished on the interstellar winds
Like motes of pollen borne upon the air;
And beings who once lived eternities
Perceived by others as a moment brief,
Like flashings of the subatomic sparks;
And others from an astral lineage
Who lived and died existences unseen
By those perceiving only matter's moulds;
And those enormous shadows over there,
Whose brows are furrowed by colossal glooms—
The ghostly pantheon of all our gods,
Whose avatars still haunt forgotten fanes
On worlds reclaimed by vast eternal night
In futile hope some acolyte of theirs
Might kindle at their altars some old faith.
Behold our ranks and files: the phantom host
That hails from sectors of the galaxy—
A spiral cluster, which, remotely viewed
From outer regions of the void, must seem
A mere amoeba in an ocean's mouth,
Whose own blind, futile gropings barely touch
The cold indifference of the universe."
The spirit legions all around me swirl
Like priests and ministers who would convene
An exorcism or some awful rite,
Discouraging my reeling mind with fear;
But speak instead the unimagined truths

Of lost religions, sciences and arts
Advanced by eon-ancient wizardries
They practiced once, and offer tutelage
In ways no sage or scholar could refuse ...
But now their eldritch whisperings grow mute;
The vision fades, and rising from the fumes
That curl in primal chaos on my mind,
I hear a mausolean ocean's roar,
And in it, all the voices of the void
Break on emergent mist-enshrouded shores,
Disperse in hissing echoes, and recede
To voiceless shallows and the gloom-fed deeps.
All's silent now; again I am alone
Amid the vapors of a vanished dream.
The chamber walls and ceiling are restored;
My body has not moved, although I feel
A distance-ravaged traveler returned
To porch and portal in transfigured night;
And by the measure of an antique clock,
I know my voyage was a moment's dream
Evolved from out of only half a glass!
I have the answer to my query now—
I must imbibe much deeper. I would know
The mysteries those hosts of ghosts would teach;
Upon the threshold of their ebon gate
I shall convoke and summon forth a guide
To lead the way beyond. Then will I be
Enlightened for a strange eternity—
Or overwhelmed by horror in the end?
I quaff the strange elixir once again
And shudder as a mist invades my mind.
Familiars! Take from me these fleshy robes,
Then heap upon them these, my ancient bones—
This sorcerer departs!

THE RHYSLING AWARD WINNERS: 1978-2011

1978	Long	Gene Wolfe	"The Computer Iterates the Greater Trumps"
	Short	Duane Ackerson	"The Starman"
	(tie)	Sonya Dorman	"Corruption of Metals"
		Andrew Joron	"Asleep in the Arms of Mother Night"
1979	Long	Michael Bishop	"For the Lady of a Physicist"
	Short	Duane Ackerson	"Fatalities"
	(tie)	Steve Eng	"Storybooks and Treasure Maps"
1980	Long	Andrew Joron	"The Sonic Flowerfall of Primes"
	Short	Robert Frazier	"Encased in the Amber of Eternity"
	(tie)	Peter Payack	"The Migration of Darkness"
1981	Long	Thomas M. Disch	"On Science Fiction"
	Short	Ken Duffin	"Meeting Place"
1982	Long	Ursula K. Le Guin	"The Well of Baln"
	Short	Raymond DiZazzo	"On the Speed of Sight"
1983	Long	Adam Cornford	"Your Time and You: A Neoprole's Dating Guide"
	Short	Alan P. Lightman	"In Computers"
1984	Long	Joe Haldeman	"Saul's Death: Two Sestinas"
	Short	Helen Ehrlich	"Two Sonnets"
1985	Long	Siv Cedering	"Letter from Caroline Herschel (1750–1848)"
	Short	Bruce Boston	"For Spacers Snarled in the Hair of Comets"
1986	Long	Andrew Joron	"Shipwrecked on Destiny Five"
	Short	Susan Palwick	"The Neighbor's Wife"
1987	Long	W. Gregory Stewart	"Daedalus"
	Short	Jonathan V. Post	"Before the Big Bang: News from the Hubble Large Space Telescope"
	(tie)	John Calvin Rezmerski	"A Dream of Heredity"
1988	Long	Lucius Shepard	"White Trains"
	Short	Bruce Boston	"The Nightmare Collector"
	(tie)	Suzette Haden Elgin	"Rocky Road to Hoe"
1989	Long	Bruce Boston	"In the Darkened Hours"
	(tie)	John M. Ford	"Winter Solstice, Camelot Station"
	Short	Robert Frazier	"Salinity"

1990	Long	Patrick McKinnon	"dear spacemen"
	Short	G. Sutton Breiding	"Epitaph for Dreams"
1991	Long	David Memmott	"The Aging Cryonicist in the Arms of His Mistress Contemplates the Survival of the Species While the Phoenix Is Consumed by Fire"
	Short	Joe Haldeman	"Eighteen Years Old, October Eleventh"
1992	Long	W. Gregory Stewart	"the button and what you know"
	Short	David Lunde	"Song of the Martian Cricket"
1993	Long	William J. Daciuk	"To Be from Earth"
	Short	Jane Yolen	"Will"
1994	Long	W. Gregory Stewart and Robert Frazier	"Basement Flats: Redefining the Burgess Shale"
	Short	Bruce Boston	"Spacer's Compass"
	(tie)	Jeff VanderMeer	"Flight Is for Those Who Have Not Yet Crossed Over"
1995	Long	David Lunde	"Pilot, Pilot"
	Short	Dan Raphael	"Skin of Glass"
1996	Long	Margaret B. Simon	"Variants of the Obsolete"
	Short	Bruce Boston	"Future Present: A Lesson in Expectation"
1997	Long	Terry A. Garey	"Spotting UFOs While Canning Tomatoes"
	Short	W. Gregory Stewart	"Day Omega"
1998	Long	Laurel Winter	"why goldfish shouldn't use power tools"
	Short	John Grey	"Explaining Frankenstein to His Mother"
1999	Long	Bruce Boston	"Confessions of a Body Thief"
	Short	Laurel Winter	"egg horror poem"
2000	Long	Geoffrey A. Landis	"Christmas (after we all get time machines)"
	Short	Rebecca Marjesdatter	"Grimoire"
2001	Long	Joe Haldeman	"January Fires"
	Short	Bruce Boston	"My Wife Returns as She Would Have It"
2002	Long	Lawrence Schimel	"How to Make a Human"
	Short	William John Watkins	"We Die as Angels"
2003	Long	Charles Saplak and Mike Allen	"Epochs in Exile: A Fantasy Trilogy"
	(tie)	Sonya Taaffe	"Matlacihuatl's Gift"
	Short	Ruth Berman	"Potherb Gardening"

172 THE 2013 RHYSLING ANTHOLOGY

2004	Long	Theodora Goss	"Octavia Is Lost in the Hall of Masks"
	Short	Roger Dutcher	"Just Distance"
2005	Long	Tim Pratt	"Soul Searching"
	Short	Greg Beatty	"No Ruined Lunar City"
2006	Long	Kendall Evans and	"The Tin Men"
		David C. Kopaska-Merkel	
	Short	Mike Allen	"The Strip Search"
2007	Long	Mike Allen	"The Journey to Kailash"
	Short	Rich Ristow	"The Graven Idol's Godheart"
2008	Long	Catherynne M. Valente	"The Seven Devils of Central California"
	Short	F. J. Bergmann	"Eating Light"
2009	Long	Geoffrey A. Landis	"Search"
	Short	Amal El-Mohtar	"Song for an Ancient City"
2010	Long	Kendall Evans and	"In the Astronaut Asylum"
		Samantha Henderson	
	Short	Ann K. Schwader	"To Theia"
2011	Long	C. S. E. Cooney	"The Sea King's Second Bride"
	Short	Amal El-Mohtar	"Peach-Creamed Honey"
2012	Long	Megan Arkenberg	"The Curator Speaks in the Department of Dead Languages"
	Short	Shira Lipkin	"The Library, After"

For a complete list of past Rhysling winners, runners-up, and nominees, see the Science Fiction Poetry Association archive at sfpoetry.com/ra/rhysarchive.html.

SFPA GRAND MASTER AWARD WINNERS

1999	Bruce Boston
2005	Robert Frazier
2008	Ray Bradbury
2010	Jane Yolen

HOW TO JOIN THE SFPA

Our members receive four issues of *Star*Line: The Journal of the Science Fiction Poetry Association*, filled with poetry, reviews, articles, and more. Members also receive a copy of the annual *Rhysling Anthology*, containing the best SF/F/H poetry of the previous year (selected by the membership), and *Dwarf Stars*, an edited anthology of the best short-short speculative poetry of the previous year.

Each member is allowed to nominate one short poem and one long poem to be printed in the *Rhysling Anthology* and then vote for the Rhysling Awards from the anthology. Members may nominate poems of ten lines or fewer to the *Dwarf Stars* editor and vote for that award as well. SFPA also sponsors an annual poetry contest and the Elgin Awards for speculative poetry chapbooks and full-length books.

SFPA Membership – One Year
$15 • PDF only for *Star*Line, Dwarf Stars, Rhysling Anthology*
$30.00 • United States
$35.00 • Canada/Mexico
$40.00 • Overseas

Ten Years
Payable in two equal payments over a period of two years (20% savings).
$120 • PDF only
$240 • United States
$280 • Canada/Mexico
$320 • Overseas
(Failure to make both payments reverts membership to the number of years equivalent to the amount actually paid.)

Lifetime
Payable in three payments over a period of three years.
$200 • PDF only
$450 • United States
$500 • Canada/Mexico
$550 • Overseas
(Failure to make all payments reverts membership to the number of years equivalent to the amount actually paid.)

All prices are in U.S. funds. Checks and money orders should be made out to the Science Fiction Poetry Association and sent to:

SFPA Treasurer
P.O. Box 4846
Covina, CA 91723

or pay online via PayPal to **SFPATreasurer@gmail.com.**